Killer Dads

16 Shocking True Crime Stories
of Fathers That Killed

By
Jack Rosewood

ISBN: 978-1-64845-079-2

FREE BONUS!

TABLE OF CONTENTS

INTRODUCTION

Welcome to **Dads Who Kill**, the true crime book that profiles 16 of the worst fathers in modern history who've killed their own families. In this book, you'll learn about how, in those cases, *Pater Familias* went deadly wrong.

When it comes to these dads, you'll find that the paternal instinct did not run so deep!

In this book, we profile some of the better-known fathers of familicide, such as Jeffrey MacDonald, John List, and Robert Fisher, but with some ideas and from angles you may not have previously read about. We also bring to you some more obscure cases, such as that of Marcus Wesson, who turned his incestuous family into a cult before killing them.

You'll read about a couple of cases that are unresolved at the time of writing—Anthony Todt and Bryan Richardson—but where the dads are accused of killing their families in the most hideous of ways.

In many families, uncles are secondary father figures to children, sometimes officially as godfathers or often unofficially when their nephews' and nieces' dads aren't in the picture for whatever reason. So, with that modern family dynamic in mind, we've also profiled two homicidal uncles who went over the edge by killing their nieces, nephews, brothers, and any other family members they could find.

These uncles clearly had no love for their extended families.

Family annihilation is the theme of this book, where the killers are those closest to the victims and entrusted with their protection. Fortunately, this is the type of situation that the vast majority of us will never find ourselves in, but it is a dark part of the world in which we live. You may think that understanding the motives of the killers could help authorities stop some of these massacres from happening in the future, but the truth is the motives of these killers were countless and varied.

Financial motives played a role in some of these cases, while in others infidelity, jealousy, and even drug abuse were factors. And in many, there appears to be no comprehensible motive.

Some people are just compelled to kill and sometimes those killers strike at those closest to them, which includes their own children.

And the backgrounds of these dads who kill are just as diverse as their murderous motives.

Dads, who kill, come from all ethnicities, socio-economic backgrounds, and different parts of the world. Some of these men may have been friends if they knew each other, but for the most part, the only thing that these 16 men share is a truly awful act of homicide they committed on their loved ones.

So now that you're prepared, sit back and read about 16 dads who won't be getting Father's Day cards.

CHAPTER 1

KILLER HIPPIES DID IT, JEFFREY MACDONALD

Nearly all of the cases profiled in this book are dads, and a couple of uncles, who without a doubt killed their entire families. The evidence against these men is overwhelming. Some were convicted in court and a few killed themselves before getting that far, yet in the process, they let the world know that they were the ones responsible for the nefarious deeds.

But of course, not everything in life is so black and white.

So, with that said, we'll start our book with a dad who killed...or did he?

Jeffrey R. MacDonald was a medical doctor and a Green Beret with a great future in front of him and with seemingly no reason to do what he was accused of doing, which to many is the most inexcusable of all crimes. MacDonald was accused, charged, and eventually convicted of murdering his pregnant wife and their two daughters at their home on February 17, 1970.

It was a horrendously brutal crime, in which Jeffrey's wife, Colette, and their two daughters, Kimberly and Kristen, had been beaten and stabbed to death. It was not a quick, painless death for the MacDonald's; they suffered through a prolonged attack before finally succumbing to their injuries. The violence was the most horrific that many of the cops on the scene had ever witnessed and to make matters worse, the details at the crime scene were even more frightening.

The word "Pig" was written in blood on the headboard of the bed of one of the dead children, eerily echoing the Charles Manson "Family" murders months earlier in Los Angeles.

It was enough to put the state of North Carolina, where the murders happened—and eventually the entire United States—on edge. Were hippies following the lead of the Manson Family by murdering random, middle-class families across the country?

It was a legitimate question that many were asking.

It certainly looked creepy and frightening, *too* eerie and frightening for the investigators. The fact that some of the details of the murders matched those of the Manson Family murders looked like a bit more than a coincidence. MacDonald even described the attack to investigators as similar to that of a murderous hippie Manson-esque group.

The investigators were immediately skeptical of that story. The fact that MacDonald had only suffered minor injuries in the alleged attack merely raised the investigators' suspicions further. Still, he was a respectable member of the community so the investigators looked at every lead...which eventually led them back to MacDonald, whom they charged with the murders. What followed was a legal odyssey that continues into the present, the most recent appeal being in 2014, with many believing that MacDonald was definitely a dad who killed, while others think he was railroaded.

Poised for Success

Jeffrey Robert MacDonald was born on October 12, 1943, in New York City to a working-class family. It was definitely a different country at that time, where people had different opportunities and different values. The idea that if you worked hard, you could get ahead in life was shared by the vast majority of Americans and was, for the most, part true. Not long after Jeffrey was born, his father followed that version of the American dream by moving the family to Long Island where they didn't necessarily have a lot of money, but where his father made do to give them a solid, middle-class lifestyle in the 1950s.

It should be pointed out here that MacDonald was not very different from many of our killer dads profiled in this book and therefore, he provides a good example with which to begin. Most of our killer dads had a similar middle-class background that seemingly set them up for success, but for some reason, somewhere, something went seriously wrong along the way.

And by every metric Jeffrey MacDonald was a high achiever in high school.

His grades were good, he excelled in athletics, and he was voted class president. He was also a blossoming ladies' man.

MacDonald's tall, athletic frame, sharp blue eyes, and charisma made him very popular with the girls. It was this popularity that would get MacDonald into trouble later in his life when he was charged with killing his family, but in the late 1950s and early '60s, it was all harmless fun. For Jeffrey MacDonald, girls came and girls went, but he was a young man on a mission. He had some pretty big goals in his life and as a goal-orientated person nothing, or no one, would get in his way.

Some say that this extreme, ambitious attitude of "taking no prisoners" played a role in his family's massacre in 1970, but in the early 1960s, it proved to be the linchpin of his success in life.

After graduating high school in 1962, MacDonald went on to study at the prestigious Ivy League school Princeton University. He had his whole life in front of him and was bound to be a success, but in the early '60s, every successful guy had to have an attractive woman at his side.

Childhood Sweethearts

MacDonald met his future wife, and many would say murder victim, Colette Stevenson, while they were attending the same high school. This is another theme that is actually quite common throughout our book with murderous dads. The killer and his wife were often childhood sweethearts, which was the situation here to a certain extent.

When MacDonald moved to New Jersey to attend Princeton on a scholarship, he studied hard but also partied hard. MacDonald continued to build on his reputation as a ladies' man, but at the same time, he kept in contact with his high school sweetheart Colette.

Colette was attending college in upstate New York, but MacDonald made trips up there to see her whenever he could.

Needless to say, it was a whirlwind romance.

The young couple threw caution to the wind, and in 1963, Colette became pregnant with their first child. Their first daughter, Kimberly Kathryn, was born in 1964, which threw the dynamics of the young couple's relationship onto a different level. Abortion was illegal at that time in the United States and wasn't really an option as they both came from traditional Catholic families. Neither was adoption considered as an option, so MacDonald decided to make Colette an "honest woman" by asking her to marry him.

She readily accepted, and the couple married in September 1963, months before Kimberly was born in April.

To Colette's stepfather and mother, Freddy and Mildred Kassab, MacDonald seemed like the perfect guy for their daughter.

"He was a nice, presentable young man. Good potential for the future, so, therefore, we saw nothing wrong with them getting married," Freddy Kassab later said about MacDonald.

And by all accounts the couple were happy. After MacDonald graduated from Princeton, they moved to Chicago where he went to medical school at Northwestern. The couple had to save all their pennies and occasionally relied on some money from their family, but he did well in his courses and they welcomed another daughter, Kristen Jean, to their family in 1967.

After graduating from medical school, MacDonald then made what some consider the strange choice of joining the Army.

Serving His Country

In 1969 the Vietnam War was at its peak, so some who knew the MacDonald's thought it was strange that the young doctor decided to enter the Army. With that said, it was the 1960s and many young men believed it was their duty to serve their country. MacDonald was always an image-conscious guy as well, and always thinking a few steps ahead, so he reasoned that serving in the military would serve him well in the eyes of the community, give him new networks to develop, and would look good on his resume.

It also didn't hurt that as a medical doctor, MacDonald's skills were quite desirable and would've certainly kept him free from any combat. His medical degree put him on the fast track to becoming an elite Green Beret and gaining a full-time posting at the Army base in Fort Bragg, North Carolina in September 1969.

For the MacDonald's family, this next phase in their lives was supposed to be their happiest. Jeffrey and Colette were still young, and his job allowed him plenty of time to spend with his wife and daughters.

But it also afforded MacDonald time to potentially get into trouble.

Despite being happily married, at least outwardly, MacDonald continued to be a bit of a ladies' man and was involved in at least two affairs. MacDonald also made a couple of enemies on base.

By 1970, the United States was consumed with a drastically rising crime rate that was at least partially fueled by drug addiction, and Fort Bragg was not immune to either scourge. According to several witnesses, MacDonald had a couple of run-ins with drug addicts attempting to get prescriptions for painkillers and opioids. When MacDonald refused to write the scripts, he was threatened by a fiending junky.

But was that enough for a junky to commit mass murder as revenge?

The Massacre

There is plenty of information available about the events at the MacDonald home on February 16-17, 1970. Books, movies, and plenty of articles have told the story. We know for certain that Colette, Kimberly, and Kristen were all brutally beaten and stabbed to death that night.

We also know that MacDonald suffered several superficial stab wounds and one serious stab wound that punctured his lung.

Most believe MacDonald committed the horrendous act, while he argues a drug-crazed hippy cult did it. Let's briefly look at both accounts.

The massacre according to MacDonald....

On February 17, 1970, at 3:42 a.m., Fort Bragg emergency dispatchers received a call about a stabbing at 544 Castle Drive. When they arrived, they were horrified at the carnage they found. According to Jeffrey MacDonald, it began for him when he was awoken from deep sleep to the cries of his wife saying, "Jeff! Jeff! Help! Why are they doing this to me?"

MacDonald claims he was sleeping on the couch in the living room because Kristen had wet his side of the bed in the master bedroom earlier in the evening.

He says that the next thing he knew he was fighting off two young white males and a young black male, with a young white woman wearing a large-brimmed hat typical of hippies of the time instigating the attacking. MacDonald says that he was struck with a wooden club and stabbed with an ice pick, but that he was able to fend off the worst of the stabs with his cotton pajama top wrapped around his arm.

Still, the attackers did a number on him and he was knocked unconscious.

When he regained consciousness, he checked his wounds and tried to revive his family members before calling the police.

The Army's Central Investigation Division interviewed MacDonald from his hospital bed, examined the scene, and looked at the forensic evidence. They came to a different conclusion.

They believe that MacDonald had an argument with his wife that night, probably over his infidelities, and after she hit him on his forehead, he snapped and beat her with a piece of wood from their bedroom closet. Kimberly then entered their bedroom after she heard the commotion and was beaten to death before MacDonald brought her body back to her own room. Then to finish off the last witness, MacDonald killed Kristen.

Although the massacre took place before DNA profiling was a reality, each of the MacDonald family members had a different blood type so reconstruction could be done of their movements.

And it was immediately clear that there were some inconsistencies with MacDonald's story.

For one thing, there were few signs of struggle in the MacDonald house. And along those lines, there were the injuries to MacDonald. Most were superficial and the one serious injury he did sustain was too good, almost as if a lot of thought was put into it.

The average person probably couldn't have given themselves a wound like that without possibly killing themselves but a person with a medical degree...

Then there was the layout of the home and the way the victims were found.

It was actually an apartment, with another family living on the floor above the MacDonald's. Neither the upstairs neighbors, nor any of their neighbors, heard or saw anything unusual that night.

If there were intruders, then they were apparently ninja-like.

Then there was the fact that despite apparently being attacked last, MacDonald was asleep in the living room, which the killers would have had to have gone through to kill the other family members. Finally, there was the fact that Kimberly's blood type was found in the master bedroom, but her body was found in her bedroom, implying that she was killed in the master bedroom then moved to her bedroom.

Not something that a drug-crazed hippy cult would probably do. And since comparisons were drawn to the infamous Manson Family murders, it's worth noting that this case didn't match up with those killings in many ways.

As brutal as the Manson Family murders were, they were also quite efficient. The Family killers eliminated every one of their victims, including a teenager in a car in front of Sharon Tate's house. If the MacDonald family killers were cut from the same cloth, it seems they would have made sure *everyone* was dead. And if they took the time to leave a message in blood, one would think that they would've taken the time to make sure MacDonald was dead, right?

And there was plenty of other circumstantial evidence pointing at Jeffrey MacDonald.

No other blood types or fingerprints were found in the house and both murder weapons were discovered by police on the back porch.

So, what about the story of the killer hippies?

Well, even in 1970, fresh off the Manson Family murder trials, people thought the story sounded a little too "neat." In fact, there was a magazine article about the Manson trial found in the living room of the MacDonald home, leading investigators to believe that was where he got the idea to blame it all on a cult.

The evidence was too much for the Army, which relieved MacDonald of his duties in April 1970 and pursued Article 32 against him, beginning in July 1970.

Article 32

In the US Army, Article 32 is similar to a grand jury in civilian courts. It is basically a trial to decide if a person will be charged with a crime and brought to trial, which for Jeffrey MacDonald, meant being charged with murdering his family.

Military prosecutors had a mountain of circumstantial evidence against MacDonald, and the horror of the crime itself. When the hearing began, it was revealed that 26-year-old Colette was pregnant and had been stabbed more than 35 times and beaten severely on the head and face.

Kimberly had also been stabbed and beaten, while Kristen was stabbed to death. Perhaps the most gripping aspect of the murder was that Kristen had apparent defensive wounds.

The case against MacDonald looked tight until defense attorney Bernard Segal called witnesses who claimed that a local hippie named Helena Stoeckley had later bragged about the murders. Stoeckley actually vaguely fitted the description of the killer, so it was a win for the defense.

MacDonald's lawyers also raised reasonable doubt by calling into evidence threats he had received from drug addicts at Fort Bragg after he'd refused to give them opioid prescriptions. It was implied that one or more of those drug addicts could have been the true killer(s) of the MacDonald family.

The testimony no doubt helped MacDonald because, on October 13, 1970, the charges against him were dropped.

But in many ways, this case was just getting started.

The Tables Turn

After Article 32, Jeffrey MacDonald received an honorable discharge from the Army and eventually moved to California to practice medicine and resume his playboy lifestyle. He even appeared on *The Dick Cavett Show* on December 15, 1970, to talk about his case.

In case you're a bit younger and reading this, Dick Cavett was *the* premier talk show host in the late 1960s and 1970s in America. Unlike Johnny Carson, who emphasized comedy on his show, Cavett often took a more cerebral approach, interviewing cultural luminaries, politicians, and even notorious criminals, so Jeffrey MacDonald was a perfect interview.

MacDonald went on the show to solidify his support, but he came off as anything but sympathetic. Less than a year after the horrific murders, MacDonald seemed to be less of a grieving father and husband and more of an arrogant jerk.

Along with millions of people, Colette's family was watching the interview and were not impressed.

"Things weren't being said right, inflections of the voice...It sickened me and it enraged me," said Colette's brother, Bob Stevenson.

It was at that point that the Stevenson-Kassab family changed their tune and began pressing federal prosecutors to charge MacDonald with murder.

Since MacDonald was never acquitted of murder - he was charged but had the charges dropped - he could be charged at any time in a federal or state court. Murder is typically a state offense, but since the massacre took place on an Army base, the Justice Department began an investigation in the mid-1970s with the Kassab-Stevenson family pushing them at every turn.

As MacDonald built a new life in California with a new girlfriend, the feds built a case against him and brought him to trial on July 16, 1979, on three counts of murder. Much of the same evidence from Article 32 was used in the federal case, and MacDonald had the same defense attorney, but two elements were very different.

Helena Stoeckley actually testified in person, but her testimony didn't help MacDonald. She appeared on the stand every bit the drug-addled loser that she was, and it seemed that she had a difficult time even understanding where she was or why she was there.

It was a big loss for the defense. MacDonald's lawyers were hoping she'd point the finger at some of her drug addict friends, but instead, she just mumbled and stuttered for a while.

MacDonald also took the stand in his own defense.

Criminal defense attorneys usually advise against their clients taking the stand, but more than likely out of arrogance, and possibly a sense of entitlement, MacDonald thought he could persuade the jury with his charisma.

The prosecution was able to expose the inconsistencies in MacDonald's original story, making him look quite unsympathetic in the process.

The jury returned a verdict of guilty on August 29, 1979.

As is the case with just about everyone convicted of a serious crime, MacDonald appealed his conviction on several grounds and was released on bail about a year later pending his appeal. After about a year and a half of freedom, though, MacDonald was returned to prison in March 1982 where he remains at the time of writing.

But the saga of Jeffrey MacDonald was still yet not over!

Fatal Vision?

MacDonald has continued to fight his case, proclaiming his innocence in the legal courts and the court of public opinion. He has exhausted all his standard appeals, although if some phenomenal new piece of evidence is discovered, there are further avenues.

Helena Stoeckley died of cirrhosis of the liver at the young age of 30 in 1983, supposedly proclaiming her guilt in the crime on her deathbed to her mother who is also now long dead.

What about DNA, you're probably wondering?

Well, MacDonald did successfully have DNA taken from underneath Colette's fingernails, but it was determined to be his, not Stoeckley's.

That final bit of evidence was the proof for most people that Jeffrey MacDonald is right where he belongs.

MacDonald has put up a good front all these years, even as he is now a senior citizen living out his final years in federal prison. He recently told a journalist, "I'm going to walk out of prison a vindicated and free man. I'm not going to walk out any other way."

Most don't believe that, including Joe McGinniss, author of the 1983 true crime book *Fatal Vision*, which is about the MacDonald case. The book, which was later turned into a TV miniseries in 1984, took the position that MacDonald was clearly guilty.

MacDonald later sued McGinniss, arguing that he was tricked into talking to the author, but the importance of the book was not so much in the rehashing of the evidence or the court testimony. No, *Fatal Vision* was important because it answered the question that many who still doubted MacDonald's guilt had: Why would a successful man with no history of violence suddenly massacre his entire family?

McGinniss argued that MacDonald was every bit the arrogant narcissist that the courts portrayed him as, and what caused him to kill was a combination of narcissism, amphetamine use, and a lack of sleep.

The reality is that Jeffrey MacDonald's case mirrors many of the others in this book - or theirs mirror his. Many killer dads were successful men with no history of violence until they snapped and killed their entire families. The evidence clearly points toward Jeffrey MacDonald as being a notorious dad who killed, but there will probably always be those who believe the charismatic Green Beret's claims of innocence and there's little chance that he'll make a death bed confession.

CHAPTER 2

ANTHONY TODT'S JOURNEY FROM FRAUD TO FAMILICIDE

On January 13, 2020, deputies with the Osceola County, Florida Sherriff's Department and federal agents arrived at the Celebration, Florida home that 44-year-old businessman Anthony Todt shared with his 42-year-old wife, Meghan and their three children: Alek (13), Tyler (11), and Zoe (4). The officers arrived to arrest Tony for defrauding several medical insurance companies of more than $130,000, but the arrest quickly turned into one for first-degree murder.

The officers immediately noticed the distinct odor of decay in the house and when they went upstairs, they found every member of the Todt family, including their dog, wrapped in blankets, dead.

The responding officers immediately knew that they had found themselves in the middle of something big.

Family members had not seen the Todts, since Thanksgiving and it had been more than a week since anyone had spoken to Anthony Todt on the phone. Based on the level of decomposition of the bodies, it was determined that Todt probably killed his family sometime around or just after Christmas.

Although many details of this case are yet to be revealed since it has not yet gone to trial, it has already taken a couple of twists and turns. What is known, though, is disturbing. It's a true example of the fact that you can never say for sure who is - and what makes - a dad who'll kill.

Triumph over Tragedy?

As the case against Anthony Todt moves forward, more information about him will be revealed, but a couple of details about what has been uncovered so far are very interesting.

Anthony was born in and spent his first four years in suburban Pennsylvania. It was a pretty ordinary life for young Anthony, until one fateful night in 1980.

On that night, when Anthony was only four years old, something happened to him that he'll never forget.

It's something that probably no one would forget!

On the night in question, Anthony was awakened to a commotion to see his mother being assaulted and then shot in the face. Somehow, she lived through the ordeal, but she suffered permanent scars and Anthony endured deep emotional scars that possibly played a role in the events that later transpired in his life.

It's hard to see how something like that wouldn't permanently affect one's psyche.

The police investigation quickly turned to Anthony's father, whom it was discovered, had hired a hitman to kill his wife. Anthony's father was sent to the state prison for a few years and his mother took the kids and relocated to Connecticut, where she remarried and started over.

It would be more than 20 years before Anthony spoke with his father.

In the years after the shooting, Anthony grew up in a relatively well-adjusted, middle-class family. He was never into drugs or criminal activity, got along well with other kids and his family, and did fairly well in school.

Still, the lingering effects of what he witnessed in 1980 were always present.

He had nightmares for most of his life and sometimes was distant from others. Todt did a good job of suppressing his problems, though, earning an MA in physical therapy from Sacred Heart College in Connecticut in 1999. It was at Sacred Heart that he met his future wife, Megan, who earned an MA in physical therapy in 2001.

The two seemed like a perfect match. They had the same interests and got along well. Friends and family all thought that Anthony and Megan couldn't have been better suited for each other, so when the couple married and began their family, it seemed like they would be a family that lasted.

And when Todt opened a physical therapy business named Performance Edge Sports in the late 2000s, the Todts appeared to be the perfect American family.

Anthony quickly built up a loyal client base and Megan worked as a yoga instructor on her own and at Anthony's clinic in East Hampton, Connecticut.

The family bought an expensive home in Connecticut and later a condo in Florida. By the late 2010s, the Todts were also renting a home in Florida as they made improvements to their condo.

On the surface, everything was perfect. But just below the surface, there was a massive storm brewing. Anthony Todt's financial success was largely a house of cards that by late 2019 was beginning to crumble.

The Walls Close in on Todt

As Anthony Todt provided his family with a high-income lifestyle, no one knew that it was all a lie funded through fraud. And I'm not talking about some fudging on tax returns regarding business expenses or some slight overbilling of clients - no, Anthony Todt was involved in fraud that may have gone into the millions.

Perhaps the most serious fraud was the more than $130,000 he overbilled to a number of health insurance companies. Since health insurance companies operate across state lines, and the health insurance industry is regulated by the federal government, Todt's little scheme brought on the attention of the IRS and the FBI to him and his company.

But as bad as that was, he was also defrauding investors of his business, some of whom were his friends.

Todt would simply accept money from investors and not pay them. The scheme wasn't particularly clever or ambitious, as there's no real way that he could have gotten away with it - other than just paying his investors back.

But he had no money to pay them.

All of Todt's money was going toward criminal defense lawyers to keep the feds at bay, and civil lawyers to fight lawsuits that were coming at him just about every day. In late 2020, he settled one lawsuit for $300,000 and owed nearly $100,000 in two other judgments against him.

And as the walls closed in on Anthony Todt, things got even worse when he lost his PT license in Connecticut and his family faced eviction from their Florida condo. Meghan and the children had been living in the condo while Anthony supposedly worked in Connecticut, but he made the trip to Florida to join them for the holidays.

It was the last holidays that the Todts would spend together.

My Wife Did It

At this point, it isn't known how much Megan knew about Anthony's financial and legal problems, or if she knew about them at all. Her discovery of the situation may have played a role in what happened next, or it may simply have been a case of Todt not wanting his family to see what a mess he'd made of his and their lives.

The Todts were last seen by family on Thanksgiving 2019. After that, Anthony said that they all had come down with the flu and couldn't talk. The reality is that sometime between Christmas and New Year 2020, he went ahead with a murderous plan that was more than likely on his mind for some time.

According to the coroner's report and the police forensic teams, Todt began his murderous rampage by poisoning his family with Benadryl, although it isn't known yet if he did so surreptitiously or if he forced them to drink a concoction at gunpoint.

A pistol was recovered from the home suggesting the latter, although statements he gave to the police suggest the former.

After the poisoning, he then went to work with two different knives.

First, he stabbed Megan twice, then Alek and Tyler once each, but he didn't stab Zoe.

To make sure everyone was dead, he suffocated them and placed their bodies on the floor of the master bedroom.

Todt then lived in the condo with his decaying family members for at least two weeks, sending occasional text messages to his sister.

Anthony Todt is now sitting in the Osceola County jail facing capital murder charges, which means that if he's convicted, he'll probably be given a death sentence. And in Florida, death sentences are regularly carried out.

So, with no conceivable defense, and facing execution by lethal injection, Anthony Todt appears to be crafting a bizarre defense that may reveal more about how he killed his family than anything.

The authorities intercepted a letter Todt sent to his father, who he had reconnected with in recent years. In the letter, he claimed that his wife poisoned the family through a laced pie.

"Long story short, she gave them the Benadryl/Tylenol PM pie, separated them, woke up at 11:30 [p.m.], stabbed and then suffocated each one," Todt wrote in a letter to his estranged father, Robert Todt. "At the news of this I ran to the bathroom and puked - I was weak."

Todt said he was gone when the murders began, and when he returned home, he found the carnage. After confronting his wife, she turned the blade on herself.

Of course, no one's buying Anthony Todt's story, but it will be interesting to see what else he will come up with to explain the murders. Based on what he's said so far, and what we know about his personality, it seems very unlikely that Anthony Todt will take responsibility for what he did. More than likely, Anthony Todt will continue to blame his wife for the murders he committed, even as they put the needle in his arm.

CHAPTER 3

STEVEN SUEPPEL, HORROR
IN THE HEARTLAND

Iowa City, Iowa is about as peaceful a place that you'll find. Located in the heart of Iowa, which is located in the heart of the Midwest, Iowa City boasts good neighborhoods, good schools, and low crime. Since it is a college town, things can get a little rowdy during the school year, and it is also a bit more socially liberal than the majority of the conservative state, but generally, most people enjoy the small city.

Steven Sueppel, his wife Sheryl, and their four adopted children also enjoyed living in Iowa City. They seemed like the perfect family: Steven was a vice president at a local bank and Sheryl was a stay-at-home mom. They were well-liked by their neighbors, their fellow church members, and were pillars of Iowa City society.

But then it all brutally ended on March 23, 2008. On that awful Easter night, Sueppel took a bat to the heads of his wife and children before ending his own life in a dramatic, fiery car crash on Interstate 80.

Sueppel left behind some notes and a whole lot of clues that explain his massacre, but most people who knew the family say they'll never be able to understand what happened that night.

The American Dream

In 2008, Steven Sueppel was a 42-year-old goal-driven family man. For Steven, his life began in Iowa City in 1965. Life was pretty ideal for

Sueppel, who did well in school and after graduating attended the University of Northern Iowa in Cedar Falls, Iowa, which is where he met his future wife, Sheryl Kesterson.

Steven was held to high standards from a young age by his parents and as he got older, he held himself to that same high standard. He strived to get the best grades and test scores in college and after college to get a good job and advance in his career. He also strove to find a high-quality wife, which is what attracted him to the beautiful and intelligent Sheryl.

After the couple married, Sheryl taught for several years and Steven worked his way up in the financial world, eventually landing a vice president position at Hills Bank and Trust in Iowa City.

The Sueppels were active in their local Catholic parish as well, and by the early 2000s, they were doing so well financially that they decided to move into the large home they needed for their growing family.

The Sueppels adopted four Korean orphans, beginning with Ethan, who was ten in 2008, followed by Seth (8), Mira (5), and Eleanor (3). Steven and Sheryl were proud of their children and the lives they had built, as evidenced by the many pictures that showed them smiling and having fun on family vacations. Yet everything the Sueppels had, was built on a series of lies and crimes.

And as long as it took Steven to build an idyllic life, it all came crashing down relatively quick.

Becoming a Crook

Much like Anthony Todt in our previous chapter, Steven Sueppel was engaged in plenty of nefarious financial transactions at work. It turns out that Sueppel had a hard time saying no to nice cars, homes, and other things. He couldn't tell his wife 'no' when she wanted to adopt more children, and he couldn't say no when she wanted to move into a bigger and newer home.

Steven liked the material comforts as well, but neither he nor his wife made enough money to keep their lifestyle. In fact, Sheryl quit working to be a full-time mom, so Steven had to increase his income.

Getting a part-time job just wasn't going to do it, so he looked around him and all he saw was money. Being the number two guy at the bank meant that he could move the ledger around from time to time, or even walk out with some physical cash occasionally.

Sueppel began embezzling from the bank in 2000 and as the years went on and he got away with it, he kept doing it more and more until he had taken about $560,000 from his employer. The embezzlement went on until he was fired in October 2007.

Then the federal indictment came in February 2008.

Steven was free on bail when Easter 2008 came, but in many ways, the jig was up. His wife now knew about his criminal activities, he was probably going to go to prison, and in the best-case scenario, he would lose everything and have to start over.

Steven Sueppel didn't want to start over.

The American Nightmare

"Here's what I see going on and for these reasons you can see why this is clearly the best choice for me and my family," was how one of the many messages Steven Sueppel left for family and friends on Easter began. He left a written note as well as voice mails for his father, brother, and former employer where he explained what he did that night and why he did it.

And it began as an apparently normal Easter. The Sueppels attended Easter mass, where Sheryl's family saw them. A friend of the Sueppels also stopped by their home for a visit at around 8:00 p.m. and after that, the massacre began.

Steven probably put the children to bed and then entered the master bedroom, where he viciously beat his wife to death with a baseball bat. As brutal as the attack was, it was also efficient, killing Sheryl fairly quick. Steven then attempted to murder his children and himself as painlessly as possible by loading them into the family van in the garage and attempting to poison them with carbon monoxide.

Somehow, though, he screwed it up.

Sueppel then reverted to the brutal method he used on his wife, killing each of his children with blow after blow of the baseball bat. One child was found in his bed, two were found together in another bed, and a fourth was discovered, a bloody mess, in the middle of some toys in the basement.

There were no signs of struggle or that Sheryl or any of the children were bound. Steven probably got the jump on Sheryl while she was sleeping and the children trusted their dad until the very end. By the time they realized what was happening, it was too late.

Steven then left several voice messages between 11:00 p.m. and 4:00 a.m. He apparently tried to drown himself in a nearby river but was unsuccessful in that attempt. In practically any other situation, Sueppel's ineptness at killing himself would've been comical, but there was nothing funny about the carnage he created that night.

Finally, at 6:30 a.m., he called 911 and told them to send the police to his home. Minutes later, Sueppel drove his car into a concrete pillar on Interstate 80 and died in a ball of fire.

Many people at Sueppel's church believe that because of what he did, he'll be engulfed in a ball of fire for eternity.

CHAPTER 4

JAMES RUPPERT RUINS EASTER

The carnage that Steven Sueppel carried out on Easter 2008 was not the first notable Easter Sunday family annihilation in American history. That dishonor goes to James Ruppert, who on Easter Day 1975 murdered 11 of his family members in cold blood. Although both Sueppel and Ruppert murdered their families on the holiest of all Christian days, that is the only major similarity in their cases.

James Ruppert is the first of two murderous uncles profiled in this book. He was said by those who knew him to be a kind and helpful person, but he never displayed the kind of fatherly love for his nieces and nephews that many uncles do. Much of that probably inherited from the fact that James Ruppert hated his brother.

Ruppert also hated his mother with a burning passion that could only apparently be quenched by murder.

Ruppert blamed his mother, and to some extent his brother, for his plethora of failures in life. Unlike Steven Sueppel, who seemingly had it made until he tried his hand at embezzlement, James Ruppert pretty much failed at everything he tried.

He failed with women.

He failed with money.

He failed at establishing a career.

There was one thing, though, that James Ruppert was quite successful at - **murder**!

When James Ruppert decided he was going to be an uncle who killed, he ruthlessly and efficiently went through the family home, dispatching everyone in a quick fashion. The massacre earned James Ruppert a spot at the top of the worst family annihilators in American history. It took Ruppert 40 years to find out what he was really good at and when he did, it was over almost as soon as it began.

Not the Cleavers

James Ruppert's early life was quite difficult, to say the least. Now that in no way justifies what he later did, or even mitigates it to any extent, but it does help to explain what was going through his confused mind when he committed the twisted deed.

James Urban Ruppert was born on April 12, 1934, near Cincinnati, Ohio. He would spend most of his life in the working-class Cincinnati suburb of Hamilton, which is also where he later committed his massacre. It was perhaps fitting that Ruppert's life began during the Great Depression, as his life was one long depression.

It had few bright spots and only seemed to get worse as he grew older.

Like many people of the era, the Ruppert's were poor and often had to pinch pennies and grow their own food to make ends meet. One of the things that the Ruppert's apparently cut back on was proper medical care for their children, as young James developed a severe case of asthma that was never properly treated.

Even if the Ruppert's did have the money, though, they probably wouldn't have spent it on James.

James' mother Charity didn't hide the fact that her oldest son, Leonard Junior, was her favorite and that she would've preferred James to have been a girl. And father, Leonard Senior, wasn't exactly a positive force in James' life either.

Leonard Senior constantly berated his youngest son, often telling him that he'd never amount to anything. The Ruppert patriarch also beat James. The abuse continued until Leonard Senior died of tuberculosis in 1947 at the age of 37 when James was just 12.

James may have thought that the abuse would die with his father, but it apparently only got worse when 14-year-old Leonard Junior became the head of the house. Leonard took over where his father left off with his treatment of James by constantly belittling and sometimes even beating his younger brother.

James Ruppert's early home life was clearly a living hell, and his situation at school wasn't much better.

Unlike his relatively tall and athletic older brother, James only grew to about 5'5 and had a small, wiry build. He was picked on by the other kids, never developed a close friendship with any boys, and never did well with girls. Well, there was one girl who took an interest in Ruppert.

Ruppert met a girl named Alma in the 1950s and the two began dating. The relationship seemed to be going well, so James introduced her to some of his family members, including his older brother. Then it happened...

The next thing James Ruppert knew, Alma, the only girl who had ever shown any romantic or sexual interest in him, was "stolen" away by his older brother. James didn't say much at the time. What could he say? He still lived with his mom and didn't have anywhere to go, so he just sat and stewed about the entire situation.

He stewed and stewed as he watched Leonard Junior seduce his girlfriend, and then to make matters worse, Leonard Junior married and had eight children with her.

The Green-Eyed Monster

By the time he was 30, James Ruppert had a laundry list of psychological problems that weren't being treated. To make things worse, he watched as his older brother married his only girlfriend, had eight children with her and was financially successful. Leonard Junior graduated from college with an engineering degree and worked for General Electric. He was able to buy a nice home in the suburbs of Cincinnati and often brought his family to Hamilton to rub it all in James' face.

Or at least that's what James' thought.

The truth is, as poorly as Leonard may have treated James when they were kids, there's no evidence that he was spiteful toward him as an adult. In fact, he loaned James some money and tried to help him find work.

But James only focused on the bad memories and did very little to turn his life around.

Well, James Ruppert did make a few attempts at being successful.

James started college but flunked out after two years and attempted a career as a draftsman but failed in that as well. He then tried to make some money in the stock market, yet lost most of his investment. There were two things that James Ruppert was good at, though: being paranoid and marksmanship.

In terms of Ruppert's paranoia, there were signs of it throughout his life, but it really became pronounced in the 1960s. After he was caught making lewd phone calls to a local library, Ruppert told people that he was being persecuted by his family and the government, who wanted to portray him as a communist homosexual.

Ruppert may not have looked like a gay communist, but to most who knew him by the early 1970s, he was certainly a weirdo.

The other thing that James Ruppert excelled at was marksmanship.

Beginning in the 1960s, Ruppert began amassing an impressive arsenal of pistols, shotguns, and rifles. He would spend hours at a time setting up makeshift shooting ranges on the banks of the Great Miami River where he mowed down bottles and cans.

James Ruppert's shooting excursions provided a welcome release from the real world that, by the mid-1970s, he began to hate more and more. Everywhere Ruppert looked, he saw enemies and people who were conspiring against him, and worst of all, some of the enemies were right in his own home.

Over the years, James had borrowed money from his brother, and he was supposed to share expenses with his mother at the house they shared, but in early 1975, both called in their debts. Charity Ruppert wanted James out of the house for not paying his fair share and Leonard Junior wanted him to pay what he owed.

On Easter Sunday 1975, James Ruppert decided to settle his debt with his mother and brother once and for all.

The Easter Sunday Massacre

The night before Easter 1975, James Ruppert was getting drunk at the 19th Hole Cocktail Lounge. It was a neighborhood bar where Ruppert felt at ease and where he was able to unwind and tell the bartenders and other regular customers about all his family problems. Although Ruppert did complain a lot about his mother, especially when she began threatening to kick him out, he never *really* showed any signs of what was coming next.

Well, there was the night before the murders when he said he was going to take care of a problem. No one at the bar thought it was a big deal, so they just shook it off...

Until the next day!

James Ruppert slept into the afternoon on Easter, and as he did, his mother, brother, sister-in-law, and their eight children came to the Hamilton home to celebrate the holiday. The children, who ranged in age from four to 17, had an Easter egg hunt and then everyone went inside for lunch.

About that time, James woke from his drunken slumber and wasn't feeling in the holiday mood, so he loaded his .357 pistol, two .22 pistols, and a .22 rifle to show everyone in the family how much he loved them.

First, he went downstairs and talked to his brother for a few minutes about politics, economics, and a few other mundane things. No one knows why he did this first. Perhaps he was thinking about backing out of what he did next, or maybe he hadn't yet decided to off his family. More than likely it was the first option. But something his brother said, or maybe something that James saw, such as the way his sister-in-law looked at his brother, set him off. He told everyone he was going to do a little target practice at the river, so when he came back downstairs a few minutes later with his arsenal, it didn't surprise anyone.

There's a chance that James still may not have done the massacre at this point, but when his brother asked, "how's your Volkswagen, Jimmy?", it caused him to blow.

James thought that Leonard Junior had been sabotaging his car, so when he asked that question, he thought it was to mock him. Maybe it *was* to mock him, but regardless, at that point, James Ruppert had had enough. Now was his time to finally get some revenge on the world that had wronged him.

Ruppert set the rifle against the wall, put down the two .22 pistols, pulled out the .357, aimed it at his brother's head, and fired. After blowing off half of Leonard Junior's head, James turned the gun on the woman who in his mind he should've had and finished her off with one shot. Charity made a rush at her demented son, but it was too little, too late. He then shot his three nieces and nephews who were in the kitchen with their parents: David (11), Teresa (9), and Carol (13).

Ruppert then moved to the living room where he coldly, yet efficiently executed the remaining five children—Ann (12), Leonard III (17), Michael (16), Thomas (15), and John (4)—proving that he was an uncle who had no love for his nieces and nephews.

The forensic examination later revealed that James fired 31 shots total, with ten of the 11 killed having headshots. In other words, James systematically went through the house shooting his victims, and then went back around again giving almost all of them a headshot to make sure they were dead.

James Ruppert then spent the next three hours in the house with his 11 dead family members. As will be discussed a bit later, we may never know what was going through his mind when he committed the murders, nor what he did during those three hours. Perhaps he felt some remorse for what he did, especially for killing the children, but on the other hand, he may have felt a certain amount of pride in what he had done.

Chances are, as with most sociopaths, James Ruppert felt absolutely nothing after exterminating the lives of his family members.

At 9:41 p.m. that evening, Ruppert called the police and calmly said there had been a shooting at the address. When the police arrived and found the carnage, Ruppert told them that "my mother drove me crazy by always combing my hair, talked to me like I was a baby, and tried to make me into a homosexual."

The police who responded to the scene were absolutely horrified by the amount of blood. Blood was splattered on every wall and dripping through the floorboards into the basement. And even worse was the overall context in which the victims were found.

Former Butler County prosecutor, John Holcomb, stated what he saw when he arrived at the scene:

"When I walked through that front door, right in the middle of all that carnage, I saw that little 4-year-old boy, with blue bib corduroy overalls on, a long-sleeve blue cotton shirt and laying on the floor at the foot of the couch, stretched out with a bullet hole in his head." He continued, "in his outstretched right hand, he had partially opened the tin-foil purple wrapper off a chocolate Easter egg. That was a sight that shook me to the depths of my soul, and I have never forgotten it."

James Ruppert was promptly charged with capital murder and booked into the Butler County Jail. It appeared to be an open and shut case, but was it?

A Mixed Verdict

Modern court systems are an interesting concept. Each country has specific rules regarding procedures and punishments and in federal government systems, such as the United States, each state or province has its own laws. Of course, murder is illegal in all court systems, but the punishments range greatly as do definitions of guilt and culpability.

In terms of punishment, thanks to the US Supreme Court's 1972 *Furman v. Georgia* ruling that suspended death sentences in the US for about four years, Ruppert wasn't facing execution for his massacre. Many Ohioans and people around the country weren't too happy with that, but the next best thing would be for him to spend the rest of his life in a tough maximum-security prison.

But Ruppert had other ideas.

Ruppert's lawyers immediately stated that they'd pursue an insanity defense, because, of course, only an insane person would commit such a horrific act. Although it has never been easy to win an insanity defense in the United States, in 1975, it was much easier to do so than today. As upset as many people were when they heard about Ruppert's planned defense, the reality is that he still wouldn't have escaped punishment. He would have been confined to a secure mental hospital until deemed fit to return to society.

Even if Ruppert did win an insanity defense, which was a minuscule chance to begin with, the odds he'd ever be released were slim to none.

But doing time in a mental hospital sure would've beaten a maximum-security prison.

Ruppert chose to be tried in front of a panel of three judges instead of a jury for his 1975 trial. After calling several expert witnesses who testified that Ruppert was clinically insane, the defense rested. The prosecution argued that the murders were the result of James Ruppert's long harbored resentments toward his brother and hatred for his mother.

The judges ruled 2-1 that Ruppert was guilty of all 11 murders and slapped him with a life sentence in July 1975.

Many in the Cincinnati area believed that they had heard the last of James Ruppert, but like most convicted killers, he appealed his conviction and sentence. Ruppert's lawyers argued that he wasn't given a fair trial in Hamilton and that the case should have been moved to a different location due to the intense media coverage in the Cincinnati market. The reality is that just about everyone in Ohio, or the United States for that matter, had heard of James Ruppert's Easter massacre, so finding a truly impartial panel or jury would be difficult.

Still, the appeals court agreed to give Ruppert a new trial.

James Ruppert's 1982 trial ended with a strangely mixed verdict. Both sides used their same essential arguments from the 1975 trial, with the three-judge panel agreeing with both to some extent.

The judges found Ruppert guilty of the first two murders he committed on that day, with the life sentence he received to be served consecutively. Then, in what many consider to be a strange turn in the case, the judges found Ruppert not guilty by reason of insanity for the other nine deaths.

What does that mean?

Well, Ruppert, who was 41 when he was convicted in 1975, had to serve 20 years before he was first eligible for parole in 1995. He was unanimously denied parole that year, and again in 2015. Ruppert's next shot at parole will be in 2025 when he will be 90.

James Ruppert will almost certainly die in prison, and probably sooner rather than later, but before he does, many people would like some questions answered.

Unanswered Questions

Since being sentenced to prison, James Ruppert has spent most of his time at the Allen-Oakwood Correctional Institution in Lima, Ohio. The prison opened in 1987 and serves as the primary institution for the Ohio Department of Rehabilitation and Correction's mentally ill offenders. Other than his parole hearings, Ruppert has remained quiet from behind bars, refusing to give interviews.

Of course, the lingering question that remains is: 'Why did he do it?'

The most obvious answer is jealousy and anger, but as the mixed verdict indicated, mental illness could have certainly played a role. Also, closely related to why he committed the murders is why he committed them on that day. If he really wanted to kill his mother, brother, and sister-in-law, he could have done it at any time. He didn't need to do it on Easter, and he certainly didn't need to murder all the Ruppert children.

So, when you think of the particular day Ruppert committed the massacre, it looks more like he did actually plan these murders for a day that would have maximum effect.

After Ruppert was sent away for life, the Ruppert home became a sort of macabre tourist stop for those who wanted to see the house where the family was massacred. The house has since been continuously occupied, with no major complaints of ghosts or violence emanating from the house.

But in a bizarre post-script, just over 20 years later, another brutal murder took place across the street in the usually quiet neighborhood.

In 1997, Timothy Bradford murdered his girlfriend in the duplex he shared with her across the street from the former Ruppert house. Unfortunately, domestic murders are common throughout the world, but this particular one made headlines because Bradford dismembered the body and scattered the parts in a nearby field and lake.

Bradford was quickly caught and given a 25-year sentence.

Almost immediately, people noticed that the brutal 1997 murder had happened just across the street from the Ruppert family massacre. The two crimes were clearly unconnected, but many people got an uneasy feeling about the street.

Maybe Minor Street in Hamilton, Ohio is cursed?

CHAPTER 5

WHEN SCIENCE MEETS SUPERSTITION, PURUSHOTTAM NAIDU

This next case is still working its way through the court system, so many details are yet to be revealed, but what is known is quite bizarre and more than worthy of inclusion in this book. On January 24, 2021, the police in the southern Indian town of Madanapalle were called to the home of Purushottam Naidu and his wife Padmaja.

They were horrified and perplexed by what they found.

The couple's adult daughters - Divya Sai (23) and Alekhya (27) - were found dead and apparently posed. Divya Sai had been beaten and stabbed and Alekhya had been bludgeoned to death. Both young women were wearing matching red saris and had their hair cut like monks.

Numerous religious items were found near the bodies of both women.

To the officers who arrived on the scene, it all seemed very strange. The placement of the bodies, what they were wearing, and their hair, all obviously represented something, but they didn't know what.

The father and mother were quickly brought in and questioned. After short interviews, they were arrested for their daughters' murders.

But the Indian police are so far unable to comprehend what they've learned.

Much of it really does defy rational explanation.

From what is known about the Naidu family, they were all quite educated. Purushottam was a chemist who was an administrator at a local teaching college. Padmaja was a former teacher. Both of their daughters were also college graduates. The Naidu family may have been well-educated and professional, but they also had some unorthodox religious ideas.

The Naidu's apparently believed that an apocalypse was inevitable and that they had to take it upon themselves to somehow survive the coming storm by doing the right thing.

For Purushottam and his wife, doing the right thing, apparently, was killing their daughters so they wouldn't be contaminated with the evil of this world. Only then could they come back to live as spiritually pure individuals in this world.

A Rational Couple?

Purushottam and Padmaja were from different towns in the southern Indian state of Andhra Pradesh, but they met in the early 1990s and shortly thereafter started their family. With a doctorate in chemistry, Purushottam had no problems finding work, eventually rising to the position of vice-principal and associate professor at the Government Degree College for Women in the city of Chittoor. Padmaja also taught at a school in Chittoor for more than 23 years. Both earned plenty of professional respect from their colleagues and were liked by most of their neighbors.

The neighbors who knew them, that is.

For the most part, the Naidu's kept to themselves. They were able to as they had a relatively large, three-storied home. It wasn't that the Naidu's were unfriendly, necessarily - at least, that's not how they were viewed - but it was more so that they were busy with their careers and family.

Over time, though, family and neighbors of the couple began to see some changes.

Both parents were devout Hindus and because Hinduism is a polytheistic religion, many different deities are worshipped. This involves just as many rituals, which to outsiders to the religion may seem strange but to Hindus, it is very logical. The Naidu's' religious devotions, though, began to get darker in recent years, focusing on elements of end times-type prophecies along with some witchcraft and magic.

Despite all of their education and seemingly rational beliefs, the Naidu's came to believe that the end times were near and that for some reason, they had to be dead to survive it!

The Kali Yuga and COVID-19

As the police sifted through the bloody crime scene at the Naidu home, they immediately noticed strong religious connections. Divya Sai's body was found just outside the family's prayer room, and then there were the matching saris and priestly haircuts that the women were wearing.

Then the police found a booklet of the writings of the guru Meher Baba next to the body of Alekhya. Meher Baba (1894-1969) was an interesting guy, to say the least. Born into a Zoroastrian family in Bombay, Baba claimed to have suddenly attained spiritual enlightenment as a young man, so he then spent the remainder of his life attempting to impart that knowledge to the world. Interestingly, Baba never spoke for the last 44 years of his life, communicating through writing and sign language.

Baba also made cryptic predictions about the future, that have never been completely interpreted by his followers.

Some believe that Baba's philosophy taught about "end times" that reflected those in Zoroastrianism, while others argue that Baba focused solely on individual enlightenment.

The Naidu's apparently took the apocalyptic teachings to heart.

To add to the religious mystery around the murders, when the police first asked Purushottam and Padmaja about what happened, they responded, "Give us till the end of the night, we will bring them back."

Padmaja added that the police had interrupted "a majestic heaven on Earth that was about to unfold."

So, as Purushottam and Padmaja cooled their heels in the local jail, the police delved deeper into the nonconventional religious beliefs of the Naidu family and discovered that Alekhya and Divya Sai were also ardent believers in what amounted to a family cult.

The central theme of the Naidu family appears to have been that the world was at the end of the Kali Yuga and that actions they took could help that come about quicker. According to the Hindu religion, time is divided into four eras, known as Yugas, which are named for different deities. Currently, we are in the era of Kali, who is the god/demon of chaos. Faithful Hindus believe that this yuga is marked by greed, corruption, and is generally evil. Once the Kali Yuga is over, though, the world will return to a golden age where humans and gods live together.

It is believed that the Kali Yuga will end when the god Shiva returns to the Earth.

In the days before her murder, Alekhya had posted several apocalyptic messages on Instagram warning her friends and followers that "Shiva is coming."

And not long before the massacre at the home, Padmaja refused a mandatory COVID-19 test at her work, claiming that the virus was part of Shiva's plan to cleanse the Earth.

The Naidu's' unorthodox religious beliefs, combined with their relative social isolation, especially after the COVID-19 virus hit, contributed to the extreme acts of violence that gripped their home on January 24.

"Screams" and "Chants"

According to neighbors, the Naidu family pretty much kept to themselves, even more so after the lockdowns of 2020 due to the COVID-19 virus.

With that said, the Naidu's were said to be good neighbors and were never a problem.

That was, until January 24, 2021.

On that afternoon, the Naidu's' neighbors were alerted to - and frightened by - the sounds of "screams" and "chants" emanating from the Naidu home. If only they knew what was happening inside.

Apparently, Purushottam and Padmaja decided that the end of the Kali Yuga was upon them, but the only way to bring Shiva to Earth was for them all to die. They would recite some prayers, which were the "chants" the neighbors heard, before committing the murder-suicides.

The couple decided to start the bloody spree with their daughters.

The violence began with Padmaja bludgeoning Divya Sai in her bedroom around 2:30 p.m. She may also have been stabbed with a trident.

As awful and strange as the attack was, the details surrounding it are even more bizarre. Apparently, Padmaja did most, if not all of the attack, with Purushottam standing by. Fathers are supposed to protect their children, but in this case, Purushottam condoned and even instigated the murder of his daughter.

But the next attack didn't happen until two hours later, which indicates that Alekhya was very aware of the situation and perhaps even accepted her fate to a certain degree. She was bludgeoned outside the family's prayer room.

After killing their daughters, the police believe that the couple planned to kill themselves but only after performing the proper rituals. Purushottam and Padmaja continued their chanting into the evening, with Purushottam only taking a break to call a friend of his at 7:00 p.m.

Purushottam's friend then called the police. The police were also called by concerned and annoyed neighbors just after 8:00 p.m.

When the police arrived, they were taken aback not only by the brutal scene but also by the behavior of the Naidu's. Both parents appeared to be in a trance and not very concerned about the condition of their daughters. In fact, Padmaja became angry with the police for being there.

"She said that we brought demons into the house when we opened the doors. She asked us to leave and come back the next day and witness the miracle that was about to happen in the house, where her daughters would come back to life," a responding police officer said.

Padmaja claimed that her daughters were in a trance and they'd be reanimated if given the chance.

The couple was interviewed, as much as a rational interview could be conducted, and they were sent to the local jail. But both of the Naidu's continued their chanting in the jail, so they were sent to a local mental health facility.

After being given plenty of medication to calm them down and apparently bring them back to reality to a certain extent, the couple realized what they'd done and showed remorse. They were sent back to the local jail where, as of April 2021, they await their trial for murdering their daughters.

No doubt Purushottam Naidu will have plenty of lonely nights in his jail cell, contemplating how his life would have been different if he'd been a true father and protected his daughters. Instead, he'll always be remembered as a dad who killed.

CHAPTER 6

WHERE DID ROBERT FISHER GO?

Our next case is pretty unique because, after nearly 20 years, it remains unresolved and, in many ways, unsolved. Although all of the evidence points toward Robert Fisher killing his wife and two children on April 9-10, 2001, there's been no closure on this case because Fisher remains at large. Robert Fisher was added to the FBI's Ten Most Wanted Fugitives list and has been profiled on true crime shows such as *America's Most Wanted* and *Unsolved Mysteries*.

Still, despite the intense publicity, it's as if Robert Fisher simply vanished.

When his car was found in a remote area of Arizona a few days after the murders, some thought the avid outdoorsman was hiding in the mountains. Others believed it was a red herring meant to throw the authorities off his track.

Because Fisher hasn't been heard from in over 20 years, many believe he died up in those mountains or perhaps that he was killed in some back alley in a developing country.

But others think Fisher had every aspect of the murders planned and is now living a life of comfort somewhere in a warm climate. After all, Robert Fisher was a controlling person who planned every little detail of his and his family's life, so why wouldn't he have planned far ahead to change his identity and start a new life?

The hunt for Robert Fisher is truly one of the greatest mysteries of modern criminal justice but unfortunately lost in that search are the three people who had their lives snuffed out by the man they trusted most. Although Robert Fisher's case may seem more exciting than many of the others, the reality is that he was just another dad who killed.

Robert Fisher was a man who needed to be in control at all times, so when he slowly began losing his grip on his family, he decided to cross the line of ultimate betrayal and kill them all. Then, instead of taking his own life like Steven Sueppel and some other dads who killed did, he simply walked away, possibly into another life. Now Robert Fisher is a fugitive for his familicide and it's anyone's guess where he is or even if he's alive.

Setting the Tone Early

Robert William Fisher was born in 1961 in Brooklyn, New York to William Fisher, a banker, and Jan Howell, a homemaker. Not long after Robert was born, the family moved to the Tucson, Arizona area, which is where he would spend the majority of his life.

By all accounts, Fisher had a pretty normal life as a kid. He had two sisters and his father was able to provide them with a typical, middle-class lifestyle. Robert especially enjoyed all outdoor activities - camping, fishing, hunting, and hiking - and there was plenty of those for him to do in the Tucson area.

Young Robert was very close to his dad, who spent time outdoors with him, but he also loved his mother. Robert was an average to above-average student and he was never a discipline problem. Everything seemed to be going well in young Robert's life...

But then Robert's parents divorced when he was 15.

Divorce is a common part of marriage in modern America and in 1976 when Robert's parents divorced, it was actually near its peak. So, he didn't become an outcast at school because of it, but it did affect him profoundly.

Instead of going to live with his mother most of the time, as is the case after most divorces, Robert and his two sisters went to live with their father full-time. Robert's father was a good material provider, but he was somewhat of a relic of the old-school, so to speak. He could be a stern disciplinarian and needed to have things done his way. Above all, William Fisher wanted order in his and his family's life.

And order became the one concept that Robert Fisher followed throughout his life. It was what drove him to became the man he was and, in many ways, it probably also drove him to murder.

Due to his upbringing that stressed order, Fisher became a bit standoffish and a loner when it came to other relationships. He never had many friends and didn't date much in his teens or early twenties. After he graduated from high school in 1979, Fisher decided to enlist in the Navy and see the world.

The order that Fisher prized so much in his life proved to translate well during his hitch in the Navy. He was promoted to the rank of a petty officer as he did his service on the USS *Belleau Wood*, which was based out of San Diego, California.

As well as Robert fitted in with Navy life, he also seemed to enjoy being in the service. He told his family that he was considering becoming a "lifer" in the Navy and that he wanted to become an elite SEAL. Despite being in peak physical condition, Fisher, like most men, just didn't have what it took to be a SEAL and quickly washed out of the unit's rigorous recruiting process.

Failing to make the SEALs was a major setback for Fisher, the second major setback of his life. But like with most things, Robert didn't say much about it to those who knew him, except in passing references. He also didn't let the failure linger very long, as he quickly rebounded after his honorable discharge from the Navy in 1982 by picking up a firefighter job in rural San Diego.

Robert Fisher was definitely a high testosterone guy, or at least he wanted to be seen that way, so fighting forest and bush fires in the hills east of San Diego seemed to be a job right up his alley.

When Robert wasn't fighting fires, he was attempting to come out of his shell to a certain degree.

By the mid-1980s, he was socializing with more people and began attending a Baptist church in San Diego, which is where he met his future wife, Chicago native Mary Cooper. The attractive blonde was immediately drawn to Fisher, who despite his occasional social awkwardness was tall, fit, and fairly intelligent. Fisher could be charming when he wanted to, which is how he was able to woo Mary into marrying him in 1987.

Robert Fisher seemed like the ideal church-going husband in 1987, but eventually, the façade he developed would begin to crumble as the ordered universe he'd created slowly unraveled.

Some People Shouldn't Have Families

Getting married and starting a family is a natural progression in life and what many people, probably most, desire. Of course, not everyone wants to have a family and there are those who do - or at least think they do - who probably shouldn't.

Robert Fisher was a man who shouldn't have had a family.

Fisher was a textbook loner who would have been better off being a life-long bachelor. With that said, Fisher had an idealized version of how life should be - marriage and children - so after he and Mary wed, the couple immediately set out to start a family.

They moved to the Phoenix suburb of Scottsdale, Arizona, where they lived not far from Mary's retired parents. The couple welcomed their daughter, Brittney, to the family in 1988, and son Bobby was born in 1991. Robert's attempt to carefully craft a seemingly perfect, orderly family appeared successful - the children did well in school and were well-behaved and the Fishers were respected members of the church.

But by the early 1990s, things took a turn.

In 1987, the man Mary had married appeared career-driven, but just a few years later, Robert seemed more interested in hunting and fishing than advancing his career. Although Robert did alright financially as a surgical catheter technician and as a respiratory therapist, Mary and her family clearly expected higher ambitions from Fisher.

And Robert Fisher wasn't exactly the caring, sensitive type either.

Robert did his fatherly duties, but he never went overboard with his emotions. Fisher was also known to be somewhat of a strict disciplinarian, which would fit with his constant attention to order, although both of his children were so well-behaved that discipline was never a problem.

Both Brittney and Bobby were good Christian children and would have done anything to make their father happy. Although neither of them enjoyed hunting and fishing as much as their father, they happily accompanied him on trips to spend time with him.

On one particular fishing trip, Robert decided to teach his kids a valuable lesson.

Neither of Robert's children had learned how to swim, so when he brought them on a fishing trip with one of his friends, he decided to teach them by "throwing them in the deep end." Literally. Robert calmly walked over to where they were sitting, picked them up one at a time, and threw them in the water. As the kids thrashed around in the water and cried out for their dad to save them, he watched on, telling them to tread water.

After a couple of minutes, Fisher pulled his children out of the water, convinced he had taught them a valuable lesson.

Preparing for the Act?

Robert Fisher was never accused of being physically abusive toward his wife or children. Some who knew him said he was a jerk, cold, and/or distant, but no one ever said he hit or beat his family members. Still, by the late 1990s, his solitary and sometimes withdrawn personality was clearly becoming a problem for Mary.

The couple began having arguments, which were overheard by witnesses, and Robert cheated on Mary with a sex worker in 1998. Although he tried to keep the indiscretion a secret for a while, he eventually came clean.

Mary agreed to look past the affair if Robert agreed to attend counseling sessions with her at their church.

Although Robert agreed to the counseling sessions and dutifully attended each session, he was just going through the motions. For Robert, who wanted order more than anything in his life and for him to control that order, the counseling sessions represented one more assault on that order and a threat to his control.

If he didn't agree to the sessions, though, his wife might have left him, taking the kids with her.

For Fisher, divorce was not an option.

It appears that Fisher wanted to avoid a messy divorce not so much for the sake of his children, but more so for himself. He told the few friends he had that his parents' divorce had left him traumatized and that he vowed to "never get a divorce."

"He was adamant about not going through a divorce or putting his family through a divorce," the family's pastor, Gregg Cantelmo of Scottsdale Baptist Church, said.

So, in light of all this, one has to think that Robert Fisher meticulously planned not only the murders of his family but also his now 20-year life on the run. It appears that Fisher made the decision to become a dad who kills in early 2001 and shortly thereafter began making his plans. He apparently found the control he had over his wife and family had slipped to the point that he thought he'd lose them, so before that could happen, he decided to end things on his own terms.

Robert Fisher was going to leave such an impact that no one would ever forget him.

Blowing It All Up

Although it does appear that Robert Fisher prepared for his ultimate act of familicide months before the event, whether or not he chose that particular day to commit his horrific crime remains a mystery. There is evidence that can point toward either scenario.

April 9, 2001, began just like any other day in the Fisher home. The adults went to work and the children went to school. Both of the kids had activities after school, so after Robert got done with his shift at the Scottsdale Mayo Clinic, he picked Brittney up at home and brought her to an award ceremony for the National Junior Honor Society. But before Brittney could be inducted into the prestigious organization, he took her and went home.

Perhaps Robert had bigger things on his mind that evening.

Mary was with ten-year-old Bobby at a gun safety class that evening, and after she returned home, the Fishers' neighbors could hear her arguing with Robert. That argument didn't last long and, that combined with the distance and the fact that the neighbors didn't want to be too nosy, they were unable to make out any of the details.

That was the last time anyone heard the voice of Mary Fisher.

The police believe that sometime after 9:30 p.m., Robert Fisher carried out his evil act.

He began by shooting his wife in the back of the head and then slashed the throats of his children from ear to ear. It's unknown if the kids were sleeping when he carried out the murders, largely because of what he did next.

Robert disconnected the gas line to the furnace in the back of the house, lit a candle, and left. At 8:42 a.m. the residents of the quiet suburban neighborhood were jolted by what was described as the sounds of a war zone. The explosion could be felt for miles and the plume of smoke it created could also be seen throughout the eastern Phoenix metro area.

It wasn't immediately clear what had happened and it was several hours before the bodies were discovered. Mary's family initially thought something bad must have happened to Robert as well, with her father Bob even pleading on live television, "Where are you, Robert? Please come home."

But Robert was a long way from the scene before the police figured out what had happened.

In addition to Robert being missing, so were Mary's car and the family's dog.

Then a series of clues put the police hot on Fisher's trail to the middle of nowhere.

An ATM security video showed that Robert withdrew $280 on the night of the murders. The police then named Fisher a person of interest in the murders on April 14. Mary's car and the family dog were found on April 20 in the Tonto National Forest in a remote area of eastern Arizona.

The clues immediately led to plenty of speculation.

Police search teams quickly scoured the mountains and caves of the Tonto National Forest but turned up nothing. One theory was that the avid outdoorsman Fisher had fled to the mountains to hide out before moving on to another location.

Some believe he did exactly that, while others think he died somewhere up in that remote area.

But many think the placement of the car was just a red herring that Fisher put out there to throw the authorities off his scent.

Those who believe it was a red herring say that the family dog probably would have followed him into the mountains, but instead, it was found waiting next to the car. This has led some people to think that Fisher had another car at the location or someone picked him up.

It's doubtful the consummate loner had help. There was a sighting of a man matching Fisher's description walking on the side of the road in the days after he was named as a suspect but before Mary's car was found.

One last thing to consider, which hasn't been given much media attention, is the timing of the murders. Fisher was born on April 13, so the murders were committed right before his birthday. It's doubtful that the timing of the murders and Fisher's birthday were a coincidence, but whether or not he planned to join them on that day or if he actually planned to be reborn, so to speak, remains to be seen.

FBI's Most Wanted

Being a fugitive is not easy. Most fugitives are captured fairly quickly and those who evade capture for years, or even months, usually have a plan. So, for Robert Fisher to have evaded capture for 20 years, without even being seen, leads one to believe that he is either dead or he did indeed have this planned.

But did Robert Fisher have the skills and background to be a successful fugitive?

Robert Fisher didn't have a criminal background, which would put him at a disadvantage in trying to survive in some pretty precarious places and positions. He wouldn't possess those intangible qualities and experiences that would help him survive on the run. For instance, he wouldn't have the experience of knowing when and how to avoid police contact. He also wouldn't know how or where to contact people in the criminal underworld to gain access to things he would need to move more freely, such as fake IDs, transportation, and weapons.

Fisher had no experience committing crimes such as burglaries for money, or a place to stay, in order to stay on the run.

Fisher also doesn't speak any foreign languages and has no travel experience or connections outside the United States.

What about Fisher's outdoor background?

Well, he may have camped out for a while, but experience shows that it's not viable to be a fugitive long-term in the wild. When Olympic Park bomber Eric Rudolph was captured in North Carolina in May 2003, he had been living as a fugitive in the wilds of Appalachia for over five years, but even in that case, he came into towns to scrounge for food.

And scrounging for food is how Rudolph was caught.

So, if Robert Fisher is still alive, which many believe he is, he has more than likely changed his identity but may be working for cash under the table. Enough important people in the FBI believe he is still alive because he was added to the Top Ten list on June 29, 2002, and remains there as of 2021.

So, if Robert Fisher is still alive, where would you expect to find him?

Sergeant John Kirkham, a Scottsdale Police officer who worked on the Fisher case, believes that Fisher is "probably living in another state and working at some menial job." Fisher does have friends and family in New Mexico and Florida, but the authorities have checked those leads and it doesn't appear that he's made contact with any of those people.

A former co-worker of Fisher's named Adam Trahan also believes that Fisher got away and has resumed somewhat of a normal life.

"I personally believe by now he's hooked up with somebody. The way he is, the way he was such a control freak with Mary, I'm sure he's found companionship. If he did find it, it's probably with a woman he's extremely controlling of."

Mary's mother Ginny also believes Robert Fisher started a new life and remarried.

A psychic named Skylar Robinson even offered her "skills" and opinion on the case:

"He lives in a trailer. He's gotten a little too comfortable in this town. He's not trying too hard to stay hidden."

By 2003, Robert Fisher's case had been profiled numerous times on *America's Most Wanted* and would continue to be on other, similar TV shows producer and host John Walsh created after that show was canceled. Each show garnered more interest in the Robert Fisher case, creating a few close calls.

Some Close Calls

The first seemingly credible report of Robert Fisher being alive came from Canada in 2004. The target matched Fisher's description, right down to a scar on his back and a gold bicuspid. After watching the man for a few days, a joint team of Royal Canadian Mounted Police and FBI agents swooped in and arrested him.

But after running the man's fingerprints through the AFIS database, they determined it wasn't the elusive Fisher.

Another tip came into the FBI that said Fisher was living in the area where his wife's car was found. Since there aren't many people who live in that area, investigators did a search of the mountains but once again did not turn up anything.

The last close call regarding Robert Fisher placed him at a house in Colorado in 2014. The police actually raided the address and made two arrests, but after interviewing the two people arrested, it was determined that they had nothing to do with Fisher.

So where does this leave the hunt for this elusive dad who kills?

You may be in the camp that Fisher committed suicide or died in an accident in the mountains shortly after he massacred his family. Or maybe you think he's still on the run. If you think Robert Fisher is still alive out there somewhere, be on the lookout for a six-foot-tall outdoor enthusiast who walks with an exaggerated upright gait due to a back injury, and who chews Copenhagen chewing tobacco.

More than anything, though, remember that Robert Fisher is a very "average" guy.

This dad who killed may be living next door to you!

CHAPTER 7

CULT LEADER AND FAMILY KILLER, MARCUS DELON WESSON

Since the 1960s, religious cults have been a fairly common phenomenon throughout the United States. Most of these groups are led by charismatic leaders who offer people disaffected with their life's answers to all their problems; in return, they only have to give the leader their complete allegiance, and usually their money as well.

The most successful cult leaders usually combine at least above-average speaking skills with an uncanny ability to see and exploit weaknesses in others. Cult leaders also usually have a fundamental understanding of world religions, which they draw from in unusual ways, as well as human psychology. And although not all cults are violent, by definition, they are all repressive.

But as twisted as cult leaders are, it's not necessarily an easy gig....

Unless you have a captive audience.

Marcus Delon Wesson is perhaps the most bizarre and sickest of all the dads who've killed profiled in this book. As strange as the theology of Wesson's cult was, integrating elements of Christianity with vampirism, it was nothing compared to whom he attracted as followers.

Instead of going out and searching for followers, as Charles Manson did, or starting a physical church and letting the followers come to him as Jim Jones did, Wesson got his followers from his own family.

But that's just the start of this sick tale.

Yes, Marcus Wesson indoctrinated many of his own children into his demented religion, but even worse, he sired many of his children *with* his children. And once Wesson's incestuous cult became public and officials began closing in, the sick dad decided to commit the ultimate evil act by killing nine of his family members on March 12, 2004.

The incident was the worst case of mass murder in the history of Fresno, California, and its impact still reverberates throughout California's Central Valley. As people look for answers to know why Wesson did what he did, though, most soon realized that Marcus Wesson was on a special level of sick and crazy that most of us normal people will never be able to comprehend.

The Seeds of Sickness

The early lives of many of the dads who kill we've profiled so far were relatively quiet and didn't necessarily point toward a future familicide. Some had disciplinarian fathers, or maybe their parents divorced, but nothing very extreme.

In Marcus Wesson's case, though, there appear to be some very visible seeds of sickness early in his life.

Immediately after Wesson committed his horrible massacre, police and journalists began digging into his past to learn what they could about this man. As some disturbing details were revealed, other important factors still remain a mystery.

Wesson was born Marcus Delon Wesson in 1944 in Kansas, to Ben and Carrie Wesson. Ben never played much of a role in Marcus' life, as he was often gone and when he was around the house, he was usually drunk. Marcus' father often took out his frustrations over his failures in life by beating Marcus, his three siblings, and Carrie.

Perhaps because of the era, Carrie never said or did anything to escape Ben's abuse. She was an ardent follower of the Seventh Day Adventist Church and raised Marcus in the church, believing that they should find solace in God and that the abuse would end if they had enough faith.

Carrie Wesson believed that everything had a reason and if God willed it, then the abuse would end.

Eventually, the abuse did end when Ben never came home one day. After weeks went by, Carrie decided to do what others in her family had done by moving with her children to California.

She hoped that the fresh start and change of environment would help her family.

California in the early 1960s was a booming place, with the entertainment, military, and energy industries providing thousands of jobs. The Wesson's settled into their new environment and for a time, it looked like Marcus might do well. He did well in school, was generally liked by the other kids and students, and was a choir boy, literally.

Despite his tough childhood, by the mid-60s, it looked like Wesson may actually do something with his life. He enlisted in the Army in 1966 and served two years as an ambulance driver. He was fortunate enough, or not, to avoid being sent to Vietnam.

When he was discharged in 1968, Wesson returned to California, which was by then a very different place.

The counter-culture movement had permeated nearly every area of California by 1968, which proved to be quite beneficial for Wesson's decades-long descent into depravity. Wesson looked around the Bay area, southern California, and even the Central Valley and saw plenty of gurus who preached alternate religions and free love. Both of those were things that interested Wesson, but he was never very charismatic, so he usually kept to himself.

And then he met Rosemary Solorio in San Jose.

Although Solorio was 13 years older than Wesson, he found the Mexican-American woman alluring and attractive. She proved to be quite pliable to Wesson's demands, but most importantly, she had a young daughter. Wesson began molesting Elizabeth Solorio in 1974 when she was just 14 years old, which is certainly sick, but even worse she was "given" to him by her mother!

Wesson officially married Elizabeth and months later they had their first child.

The couple would eventually have ten children of their own, and their family was augmented by children Wesson had with some of *his* children (we'll get to that in a minute), as well as several nieces and nephews. Maintaining such a large family is expensive, though, so how did Wesson afford it?

The evidence shows that Wesson was resourceful if nothing else. He and his family lived on a houseboat in northern California for a time, and when that didn't work out, they all camped in tents in the Sierra Nevada Mountains. They stayed in abandoned homes and occasionally would live in places rent-free in return for work.

Wesson rarely worked. He is known to have worked at a bank briefly after he was honorably discharged from the Army, but he quit working not long after meeting Solorio. The Wesson's survived on food stamps quite often, and to supplement their diet, Marcus would send his kids to dumpster dive or beg for food.

Marcus Wesson's family certainly wasn't the most lucrative cult in American history, but it was one of the sickest. When the details of Wesson's depravity were revealed, even the most hardened types got squeamish.

No doubt you will too!

Keeping it in the Family

Like many notorious cult leaders throughout history, Marcus Wesson used sex as a weapon to control his followers and claimed sexual rights over them. What makes Wesson different from Charles Manson or Jim Jones, though, is that all of Wesson's followers were his family members.

It didn't matter to Marcus Wesson. He had sexual relations with his children, his nieces, and even had children with some of his children.

Age and sex also didn't matter to Wesson. He molested his prepubescent family members as well as his teenage and adult family members. And although Wesson didn't sexually molest the boys in the family, he did physically and mentally abuse them in many different ways.

His son Adrian Wesson said that sometimes he was beaten so badly that he couldn't walk for a week, and his brother Serafino later reflected:

"If I had ever talked up to him or tried to stop anything he did, I would not be alive today."

Wesson acquired more victims, and followers when his wife's sister brought her children to live with them. There were eventually 16 children in the Wesson family. The abuse of the children and the cult-like status of the family began in the late 1970s, so then why did the state of California never catch wind of any of Marcus Wesson's depravity?

Well, Marcus constantly moving them certainly played a role, although he did end up in jail in 1990 for welfare fraud. That would have been the chance for the state to do a routine check on his children's living conditions, but unfortunately, the Wesson's "fell through the cracks" as they say in social worker parlance.

Another thing that Wesson did to avoid detection was keeping his children out of school. Keeping cult members isolated from the outside world is straight out of the cult leader playbook. He officially "homeschooled" his children, but as we'll see in a minute, the only education Wesson's children received was in his bizarre religion.

When Wesson's oldest children became the legal age to work in the late 1990s, he sent them to find jobs to augment the food stamps and public assistance he was receiving. It was also during the 1990s that Marcus Wesson was influenced by current events to move his family in a different direction spiritually.

Writing His Own Bible

When the Waco siege and later massacre happened in 1993, Marcus Wesson was glued to his TV set and consumed whatever news he could about the Branch Davidians and David Koresh. Wesson was enthralled by Koresh and the Davidians, not so much their theology, but more so their way of life and the perceived hold Koresh had over the group.

Marcus Wesson wanted to be his own kind of David Koresh.

Unlike Koresh, Marcus Wesson wasn't particularly charismatic, or intelligent, but he did possess a captive audience in his family, which he already ran like a cult. So, throughout the 1990s, influenced to a certain degree by the Branch Davidians, Marcus Wesson set out to write his own Bible, which combined Christianity and vampirism and condoned such unnatural acts as incest and pedophilia.

Throughout the 1990s, as Wesson physically, sexually, and mentally abused his children, nieces, and nephews, he developed a theology that would justify the depravity that he enjoyed so much. He focused on particularly violent passages from the Old Testament and he was drawn to the parts in the gospels where Jesus told his followers to drink his blood.

To Wesson, that was a sign that Jesus was a vampire.

And as time went on, Wesson began telling his family that he was Jesus and God and that they should refer to him as such.

His family members were only allowed to leave the house to work, and they weren't allowed to make friends or bring any of their coworkers to the Wesson home. When they left the house, the women always wore black skirts, white or gray blouses, and black high-heeled shoes.

When Wesson's children (we'll just refer to everyone in the Wesson house as his children, including his nieces, nephews, and other adults of the family) weren't working or listening to one of his bizarre Bible lessons, they were required to do work around his house, which included cleaning his long, dirty dreadlocks.

And of course, Wesson demanded sexual favors from his children beginning at about age eight.

Wesson eventually sired children with two of his daughters and three of his nieces.

Incest and pedophilia are what make this case the most difficult for most people to understand. Even the most hardened criminals regard pedophiles as the lowest of the low and very few cults have ever condoned pedophilia and incest. But Marcus Wesson codified both of the practices into his religion.

Beginning in the late 1990s, Wesson began writing some of his ideas in a series of notes that basically became his own Bible. He sometimes referred to himself as "Jevammarcsuspire," which was believed to have been an amalgam of the names and words "Jesus," "Marcus," and "vampire."

Wesson eventually titled his magnum opus *In the Light of the Light for the Dark* and although it will never win a Pulitzer prize, or influence millions of people like other religious texts - or probably even be published - it does shed light on Wesson's sick mind.

On his theological defense of incest, Wesson wrote: "incest one produces the seed of perfection of one's self."

He also wrote that the molestation he doled out to the young members of his family was a form of "loving," and as his niece, Rosa Solorio, later testified: "He did it so we would be better women."

Wesson was able to keep his twisted world away from the outside world for decades, and in the early 2000s, he used the money his family members made working to buy an office property in the city of Fresno, California.

If you're not familiar with it, Fresno is far from the politically liberal, cosmopolitan cities of San Francisco and Los Angeles. In fact, it's as far from that as you can get in California as far as major cities go, well except for possibly Bakersfield. Compared to most other cities in California, Fresno is not a good place to start a cult.

So, with that in mind, it should've been no surprise that the Wesson's Fresno neighbors began to wonder about the strange "family" in the former office building.

The city received complaints and eventually, the Wesson's found themselves in the middle of a legal fight for living in a location not zoned for habitation.

Marcus Wesson knew that it wouldn't be long before the officials with the city of Fresno and Fresno County would come knocking at his door and break up his little cult. In an effort to beat the officials, Wesson planned to move all his children to Washington state where his mother lived. However, before he could, two of the women who had got out of the cult decided to come back to get some of the others.

That's when Marcus Wesson made the plunge to become a dad who killed.

Not Going Quietly

The Wesson family wasn't always as tight as he would've liked it to have been. In early 2004, two of Wesson's nieces with whom he had sired children, Ruby Ortiz and Sofina Solorio, made the major step of breaking the madman's grip. Once the two women were away from the home, the world immediately looked very different and they realized that everything they had been taught from childhood by Wesson was not only wrong but also very sick.

When the women heard that Wesson was moving his family north, they knew that they had to make a move. If they didn't, they might never see the children again.

So, on March 12, 2004, the two women, along with other members of the extended family, went to the Wesson compound to retrieve as many of the children as possible.

But Marcus Wesson wasn't having it. He called them "Judas," "whores," and "Lucifer" and let it be known in no uncertain terms that he wasn't going to relinquish his children.

The women said they'd return with the police.

Over the next couple of hours, Marcus Wesson felt the walls closing in on him like no other time in his life. Not only was he about to lose his family and only source of income, he'd also more than likely be headed to prison, possibly for the rest of his life, for all the abuse he'd dished out to his children.

So, Marcus Wesson did what most cult leaders have done in similar situations and prepared for the end.

Perhaps thinking he was another version of David Koresh—who with his followers held off the ATF and FBI for months at their compound outside Waco, Texas - Marcus Wesson decided to commit to his own standoff in a small, junky, run-down office building in the middle of a poor Freson neighborhood.

Wesson's standoff wouldn't elicit the sympathy that the Branch Davidians received, nor would it be as apocalyptic, but it ended up with a massacre, nonetheless.

He cleaned his Ruger .22 caliber pistol and gathered his family in one room. Those assembled included two of his daughters with whom he'd had children with, Sebhrenah (25) and Elizabeth (17). The children were Illabelle (8), Aviv (7), Johnathon (7), Ethan (4), Marshey (1), Jeva (1), and Sedona (1).

It remains a mystery what Wesson told his family because none of them survived and Wesson left no record of the final conversation. More than likely, he told them that everything he had pumped into their brains for the last several years was about to become true and the only way out of it was through group suicide.

But first, Wesson went outside to speak with the police.

The police say he didn't say much to them, other than they should wait outside and he'd return shortly.

Then Wesson went back into the home and carried out the worst mass murder in Fresno's history. He shot each of his victims once through the eye. Since there were no signs of struggle, even by the two oldest victims, it appears they all went along willingly with the plan; to the extent that brainwashed members of an incestuous cult can do anything willingly.

After killing all nine of his family members, Wesson then piled them in a room with ten antique coffins. The number of coffins indicates that Wesson may have intended to join his family, or at least that he told them he would. But when it came down to it, Wesson was pretty much just a coward.

He was even too cowardly to have the cops do the deed.

After killing his family, Wesson quietly went outside the house, covered in blood, and surrendered. He was promptly brought downtown and charged with capital murder.

Could It Have Been Avoided?

Wesson's case immediately made headlines across the country but was somewhat overshadowed by the Laci Peterson murder case. Wesson was given public defenders, who despite having little money for experts and having such an odious client, put up a pretty spirited defense.

The defense argued that Sebhrenah actually committed all of the murders, which they supported by pointing to the fact that the gun was found next to her and her DNA was on the gun.

The prosecution countered by saying that Wesson simply placed the gun there after committing the murders and wrapped her hand around it. She also had access to the gun numerous other times and could have handled it then. The prosecution added that even if Sebhrenah was a semi-willing follower of the murder-suicide plot, Marcus Wesson was the brains behind it all.

On June 17, 2005, the jury agreed with the prosecution, finding Marcus Wesson guilty of nine counts of first-degree murder and 14 counts of forcible rape and the sexual molestation of seven of his daughters and nieces. He was sentenced to death ten days later.

But the chances of Marcus Wesson being executed are slim to none.

Despite the people of California voting against referenda to repeal the death penalty in 2012 and 2016, Governor Gavin Newsome declared a moratorium on executions in 2019. Not that it mattered anyway since the last execution was done in 2006, so Wesson has a long line in front of him.

Yet, as Wesson cools his heels in the condemned cellblock in the notorious San Quentin prison, there are many, many questions about this dad who killed, especially: Could this massacre have been avoided?

The simple answer is yes. There's no doubt that the authorities had plenty of chances and would have been justified taking Wesson's children from him. The problem is, though, it seems that none of the bureaucrats who came across Wesson wanted to deal with the problem.

When Wesson was convicted of fraud in 1989, he wrote the judge a rambling, 80-page letter that claimed the welfare department illegally obtained his information because he was using the name of famous actor Richard Widmark, and the boat the family was living on was supposed to be in his wife's name. One would think that such revelations would have warranted more investigation and charges, but they didn't.

The state also dropped the ball when it came to Wesson claiming to homeschool his children. Generally speaking, parents who homeschool their children have to show proof of lesson plans, tests, and other curriculum-related materials to operate. There are no signs that anyone from the state of California ever checked in on Wesson's lessons.

Finally, on the day of the massacre, after the police arrived at the Wesson home, they called the city attorney for permission to kick the door down and take Wesson. The city attorney said his hands were tied and they'd either have to wait for a warrant or until he came out of the home.

Marcus Wesson came out of the home covered in his family's blood and entered the murderous fraternity of dads who kill.

CHAPTER 8

HONOR KILLING IN AMERICA, YASER ABDEL SAID

So far, we've seen that religion has played an important role in the lives of many of our dads who kill. Some were controlling men who found comfort in the order and tradition that religions can bring, while one fashioned a bizarre world-view based somewhat vaguely on established religions.

Two of our paternalistic killers even chose the holiest day on the Christian calendar to commit their horrible acts.

Our next case of a dad who killed also involves religion and the little-known phenomenon, at least in the West, of "honor killing."

You've probably heard the term honor killing recently in a news report, or possibly you've read about it in a book or magazine article. The term itself is a bit amorphous and difficult to define. In its broadest definition, an honor killing is simply a murder done to avenge someone's honor. But in the context of our next case, and as it relates to most cases you hear about on the news, honor killings are done by a family to avenge what they see as their *family* being dishonored.

Most honor killing cases take place in Muslim families, although there are other known cases from other religions. Also, most honor killings involve the aggrieved family seeking to protect the honor of a female relative. The cases usually involve the female family member dating or having sex with someone not approved of by the family, often someone from another clan, ethnicity, or religion.

The victim is often the female family member who committed the "transgression," but sometimes the person with whom she is committing the act, is also the victim.

Our next case involves an honor killing by an Egyptian cab driver named Yaser Abdel Said. Said immigrated to the United States, married an American woman, and started a family. By all accounts, Said seemed to be integrated into the mainstream American fabric, but he still held tight to some of his more traditional ideas.

As his daughters grew older, they became standard American teens, which angered Said to no end.

Eventually, when he had enough, Said decided to do his own version of an honor killing.

The Angry Cabbie

Yasser Abdel Said was a rather unexceptional man. He wasn't particularly good-looking, intelligent, or charismatic. He also didn't come from a family with money or political connections, but he was a hard worker.

When Said set his mind to do something, more often than not, he followed through with the plan. And in the early 1980s, Yasser Abdel Said planned to immigrate to the United States to realize his dreams. His life in Egypt wasn't necessarily terrible; he wasn't oppressed by the government and his life was never in danger.

But his options were limited and when combined with the fact that several of the men in his family were emigrating to the United States, he saw moving there as his best chance for financial and social success.

In 1983, Said was finally given the opportunity when he was awarded a student visa to study in the US.

Yasser's three brothers and a sister followed him in his journey not long after.

College was a bust for Yasser, but he was able to maintain his visa and ended up staying permanently, gaining American citizenship in 1997. But things in the "land of milk and honey" were usually anything but, for the Egyptian immigrant.

About the only "skill" Yasser had was driving a cab, which he did as a full-time job for most of the 1980s, '90s, and into the 2000s. Although you can make some good money driving a cab, it tends to be hit or miss type work, so you always have to save money for those "miss" days, which can turn into weeks or even months.

So, to supplement his cabbie income Said worked at convenience stores owned by his family members in the Dallas-Fort Worth area. Said worked hard at all his jobs, but they only seemed to build resentment in the Egyptian immigrant. You see, his three brothers had become financially successful since immigrating to the United States, buying convenience stores and other businesses.

So Said drove his cab throughout the DFW metroplex, angry and resentful.

He thought life in America would be much easier and that he would be a success in no time. Many people who come to the United States, especially from developing countries, often have this belief and are often let down when they find out it isn't true.

But at only 30 years old, Said still had a lot of life in front of him and plenty of opportunities to make a name for himself.

Things seemed to change for Said when he was working at a convenience store in 1987 and he met Patricia "Tissie" Owens. Owens was a 15-year-old, overweight, native Texan Christian girl; not someone you would expect to end up with a guy like Said. Actually, Owens was engaged to one of Said's brothers, so when he broke it off, Said stepped in to fill the void.

After only knowing each other for one week, the couple decided to wed. The hastiness of the relationship may have had to do with Said's visa expiring within a week, but it should also be pointed out that in traditional Islamic culture dating is for the most part *haram* or forbidden.

Said did have one major obstacle to overcome before he could marry Tissie - her parents.

Even in 1980s Texas, 15 was below the age of consent, so Said would have to get Tissie's parents to sign legal papers allowing the marriage.

The couple married in a Christian church but soon after moving in together they lived a very Islamic lifestyle. Tissie gave birth to a son, Islam, in 1988, a daughter Amina in 1989, and a daughter Sarah in 1990. Said also had a daughter with another woman before he married Tissie in 1987.

Once Said had his family complete, one would think he'd be a happy man. However, as time went on and elements of modern American culture began seeping into the family, he became even more enraged.

American Wife and American Daughters

Yaser Said never really grew accustomed to life in the United States. In fact, just about all his statements and actions seem to indicate that he didn't really like the country or the people. Said wanted the material wealth and comforts that the United States could offer without having to accept the people or the culture.

He truly was an angry little man: Angry over his brothers doing better than him and angry that he never got to truly have the 'American dream.'

But the reality was that he married an American woman and had three American children with her.

By all accounts, his son was by far his favorite. Islam could do no wrong in his father's eyes and was said to be a bit of a spoiled brat. Amina and Sarah were viewed more as Yaser's property than anything else. He hoped that they could possibly bring him a change in social status by marrying them off to Egyptian men from well-to-do families. Both girls were attractive, especially Amina. Her light eyes and fair complexion would attract many wealthy suitors from Egypt.

As Yaser was attempting to set his daughters up with wealthy men, though, his marriage to Tissie fell apart.

By the late 1990s, Yaser's cab income was sporadic at best and since Tissie was a high school dropout, she could only find minimum wage jobs to supplement the family income. The tensions in the Said family were so thick they could be cut with a knife, but in 1997, they were temporarily relieved when Tissie left the family.

Amina then accused Yaser of sexually molesting her. The Hill County, Texas Sheriff's Department did investigate the claim but never made an arrest and no charges were brought against Yaser.

Sexual assaults can be difficult to prove and, when a couple is going through a breakup, accusations are not uncommon. Sometimes one of the parents will "coach" a child to make an accusation, or sometimes false accusations are made as a cry for help or to get attention.

The local authorities just didn't find enough evidence to corroborate the accusations so charges were never filed.

Tissie then did something seemingly unthinkable, but what experts would say was a sign of Stockholm Syndrome: She moved back in with Yaser in 1998. And once more the girls accused Yaser of sexual abuse, which he responded to by accusing Tissie of forging a check.

Needless to say, by the end of the '90s, the Saids were not one big happy family.

But they were a family that persisted, nonetheless. Charges were never filled against anyone in the Said family, and by the early 2000s, they had apparently worked through much of their problems.

Yaser Said would face bigger problems in the 2000s.

His son was diagnosed as mentally disabled, which was certainly a blow to the patriarchal Said. Despite the setback Islam's disability posed to Said's ambitions for his family, however, it brought in some extra cash to the family in government disability payments.

The girls, though, were teenagers by the mid-2000s - American teenagers - which presented an entirely new set of problems for the angry Egyptian cabbie.

Honor Killing in Texas

As Amina and Sarah grew into teenagers, they became attractive young women, catching the eyes of plenty of boys in the area. Yaser Said wanted nothing to do with that, so he relentlessly controlled his daughters' movements, requiring them to check in with him by phone. Later, he took their phones when he learned they were using them to communicate with boys.

By the middle of 2007, both of the Said girls had boyfriends.

The relationships the Said girls were involved in were pretty harmless and innocent, though. There's no indication either girl was sexually active, which would've been difficult with Yaser lurking around every corner. But he couldn't be everywhere.

The girls were allowed to go to school and Amina even took Tae Kwon Do lessons at a local dojo. It was there that she met a boy named Joseph Moreno, who would be her one and only love.

As Amina and Sarah made clandestine visits to meet their paramours, Yaser was coming up with a few plans of his own. He kept in contact with his family and friends in Egypt and arranged for Amina to marry a much older Egyptian man from Yaser's native region of the Sinai.

Amina refused but was beaten by her father. Actually, by the time she was 16, Amina was regularly beaten by her father for disobeying him, namely for sneaking around to be with Moreno. So, when Amina learned that her father was going to marry her off to some older Egyptian guy, she didn't have many options. She was doing well in school and was offered an academic scholarship to attend Texas A&M University.

But first, she had to get there!

On December 26, 2007, Amina, Sarah, their boyfriends, and Tissie all fled the Said home while Yaser was at work. The group didn't have much of a plan other than to escape the reach of Yaser, so they first went to the tiny town of Attica, Kansas where Tissie had some family. The group then went to Tulsa, Oklahoma to stay with some of Moreno's relatives.

The group's short-term plan was simply to escape Yaser. They would deal with the long-term implications later.

Yaser Said had some short-term plans of his own.

As soon as he noticed his family was gone, he began calling Tissie, demanding then begging her to return with the girls. When threats didn't initially work, Yaser used some charm and convinced Tissie to bring the girls home and that he'd forgive everyone.

For whatever reason, Tissie agreed and told the girls on December 31 that they were all going to take a short-day trip down to east Texas to put some flowers on her mother's grave. As Tissie drove the girls into the DFW metroplex, they knew they had been duped. Sarah agreed to return to the Said home, but Amina refused and went to a friend's house.

Tissie was persistent, though, and on January 1 convinced Amina to meet with her father.

It was the last time she'd ever see her daughters.

When Amina arrived at the Said home, she was initially scared, but Yaser put her fears to rest partially with his abnormally calm attitude. Instead of being angry, like he usually was, Yaser actually smiled and said he wanted to bring his daughters out for lunch and talk about their issues.

The only talking Yaser wanted to do, though, was with his gun. He was done dealing with his daughters and he was sick of the "shame" they were bringing to him and his family. To Yaser Said, there was only one way to deal with his disrespectful, American daughters.

He parked in the parking lot of a motel, pulled out his pistol, and began putting round after round into his daughters. Yaser then calmly walked away from his cab, and his former life, leaving his helpless daughters to bleed to death.

Sarah managed to call 911 on her cellphone to say, "Help, my dad shot me! I'm dying, I'm dying!"

Both girls were dead when paramedics arrived minutes later.

The killings caused quite a stir in the DFW area and among the Said and Owens families. The funerals of the girls were indicative of the division, with there being both a Christian and Muslim service. At one point, one of the girls' aunts said to the Muslim cleric officiating, "This was an honor killing...Don't deny it!"

The tensions between the families and throughout the greater community were only made worse by the fact that Yaser Abdel Said was officially a fugitive and supposedly no one knew where he was.

Hiding in Plain Sight

The next phase of this story of a dad who kills reflects that of Robert Fisher's case in many ways, and could actually tell us something about where Robert Fisher may be. As in the Robert Fisher case, Yaser Said left his car - which also happened to be a crime scene - for the authorities to find after he disappeared.

The immediate fallout from the murders was confusing, to say the least.

Tissie said little about the murders, although she did manage to state that Yaser was "a good man." Most of her family members disagreed.

Yaser's family members also continued to defend him, but made a point to state that the murders were in no way "honor killings." They claimed that the murders had nothing to do with Islam and that Yaser had just 'snapped' one day. Yaser's long history of abuse and desperate clinging to his traditional, 'old world ways would seem to indicate otherwise.

Most of Yaser's family appeared more concerned with defending him and the religion of Islam than grieving for the loss of the girls.

What was known about Yaser's immediate flight, though, was that he was carrying an Egyptian passport and would probably be headed to his home country.

But leaving the United States as a fugitive is easier said than done.

Although Yasser had a legitimate, current Egyptian passport, it was 2008, the post-9/11 world where computer databases check most people - especially those from certain countries - entering and leaving the United States. No doubt Yasser's passport was flagged by Homeland Security and since Yaser didn't have a criminal background, it would've made it difficult for him to obtain a new, forged, or fake passport.

Remember back to the problems we discussed Robert Fisher would encounter by not having a criminal background? Yaser Said would've faced many of those same problems, although he would have the benefit of being part of an ethnic community that may help him first and ask questions later.

He also had a large, extended family, in the US and Egypt, who seemed eager to defend him.

And the Egyptian authorities claimed that he never entered their country on his valid passport, which left the girls' American family at a dead end.

They raised more than $20,000 for Yaser's capture, which did help to keep the case in the spotlight. Tips came in that he was driving a cab in New York City, New Jersey, and Cairo, Egypt, but none of them led to his capture.

It was as if Yaser Said was a ghost.

Maybe he was dead?

Maybe he had plastic surgery?

Maybe he was living somewhere no one expected?

All of these questions remained unanswered for 12 long years. On December 4, 2014, Said was added to the vaunted "FBI's Ten Most Wanted" list, which generated some more tips but not an arrest.

In the meantime, life went on for the rest of Said's family. The developmentally disabled Islam actually came out alright, as he inherited the family home and then had it renovated with donations from the local Islamic community, Kroger supermarket, and the local public high school. He then had a bride imported from his father's native Egypt.

Islam eventually sold the house and moved into an apartment in Bedford, Texas, which is where the authorities caught their big break in the case.

On August 14, 2017, as he was doing some routine work, a maintenance worker at the apartment complex noticed an older man inside Islam's apartment. He didn't think anything of it until a week later when he returned to do some more work at the apartment and was greeted by a tall Middle Eastern man. Since the worker didn't know of any man being on Islam's lease, he told his boss about the incident.

The boss knew who Islam was and all about his family's sordid past.

The FBI immediately began their surveillance of the apartment but as they moved in to make an arrest, they just missed Yasser. They almost missed Islam as well. Islam was detained trying to cross the US-Canadian border by land, but since all the evidence indicating Islam was harboring a fugitive was circumstantial, at that point they had to release him.

But the FBI continued its surveillance.

In August 2020, the FBI tracked Islam to the home of one of Yaser's brothers, Yassein, in Justin, Texas.

Finally, on August 26, 2020, the FBI moved in and arrested Yaser Said for the capital murders of his two daughters. He faces the death penalty, which in Texas means that if convicted, he will probably be sentenced to death and will be executed by lethal injection.

Two days after Yaser was arrested, Islam and Yassein were charged with the felonies of harboring a fugitive and conspiracy to obstruct justice.

On the arrests of Islam and Yassein, U.S. Attorney Erin Nealy Cox said:

"In concealing Yaser Said from arrest, not only did these men waste countless law enforcement hours in the hunt for a brutal fugitive, they also delayed justice for Sarah and Amina. Thankfully, their day of reckoning has finally arrived. We are hopeful all three arrests will bring a measure of comfort to the girls' mother, relatives, and friends."

Islam pleaded guilty to harboring a fugitive and Yassein was found guilty of the charge. At the time of writing, both men will be sentenced in federal court in June 2021.

The final chapter of this case will only be closed when Yaser Said goes to trial. But when you consider the mountain of evidence against him, and the fact that the case is in the law-and-order state of Texas, chances are that this dad who killed will breathe his last breath strapped to a gurney on Texas' death row.

CHAPTER 9

BURNING WITH HATRED, ROWAN BAXTER

When most people think of Australia, images of sandy beaches, palm trees, and plenty of sun often come to mind. But, when they think of Australians, most tend to see them as friendly and fit people. All of that is certainly true to a certain extent. Australia is known for its warm, mild climate and its people are generally friendly and fit. Australians usually score above average in most health metrics when compared to other industrialized countries and in international sports competitions, they usually outdo their relatively smaller population per capita in total medals and victories.

Perhaps owing to a combination of the climate and higher fitness levels, Australians are generally rated as happier than most people from other industrialized nations as well. There are of course other factors that contribute to Australians being happier people on average, including lower crime and unemployment rates.

With all of that said, Australia does have its problems.

Crime can be a problem in some of Australia's largest cities, but most of that is relegated to drug and gang activity, which rarely spills over into polite society.

But occasionally there are awful crimes that burnish the image of the idyllic continent-nation, such as when Rowan Baxter murdered his family in early 2020.

Rowan Baxter was in many ways a typical Aussie: fit, good-looking, and a real charming guy when he wanted to be. By 2017 Baxter seemed to have it all, a beautiful wife that he owned a gym with and three great children. They seemed like the picture-perfect Australian family, taking vacations to the ocean and exercising together, always smiling and laughing in every family picture.

Things change, though, and for the Baxter's, several events brought their marriage to an end by late 2019. Rowan's wife Hannah wanted to make the split amicable, but Rowan had other ideas.

On a warm morning in February 2020, Rowan made one last attempt to win back his family, but it all ended in a fiery inferno. Baxter was in the process of losing everything he'd built over the last several years, so he decided that if he had to suffer losing everything, then so did his entire family. He made the ultimate choice to become a dad who killed, and then took his own life in a very dramatic fashion.

Full of Testosterone

Rowan Baxter was a natural-born athlete. Born and raised in Tauranga, New Zealand, on the island nation's North Island, Baxter came from an athletically gifted family where success on the field was equated with a good life off the field. Born in 1979, as a young boy Baxter gravitated toward New Zealand's most popular sport of rugby, which requires plenty of athleticism, hard work, and mental and physical toughness to be successful.

Rowan's older brother Charles proved to be a success and someone for him to emulate.

Charles Baxter played professionally in Rugby Sevens professional league from 2003 to 2007. It was certainly something for Rowan to look up to, but he also wanted to do even better than his brother.

As a teenager, Rowan worked hard to develop a feel for the game of rugby, although for him it really seemed to come naturally. Rowan also spent a lot of time off the field perfecting his game by hitting the gym and watching endless hours of rugby matches. It all paid off, as Rowan was *the* player at his high school, and upon graduating he made the leap to enter the pros.

Rowan got his start playing rugby union, which is one of the main two forms of rugby. He continued to work hard and in his mid-twenties converted to the other main rugby code, rugby league. Baxter earned a coveted spot on a team in the National Rugby League (NRL), the top professional rugby league competition in Australia and New Zealand.

Unfortunately for Baxter, though, his professional rugby career was over before it really started. He never played an NRL game, but Baxter used his sharp mind and connections to start a new career.

Establishing Himself

Baxter's time as a professional athlete was brief, to say the least, but he did put his time in the NRL to good use. He married, made some important contacts, and saved a little money. It was on the last point that, other than fitness, Baxter showed a real talent for.

Instead of blowing the money he made playing rugby on women, booze, and expensive cars, Baxter decided to use his earnings to become a fitness professional. He was known to be frugal and friendly, yet somewhat solitary. Baxter was never one for parties or womanizing, although he did make his rounds on the social circuit to make and maintain his professional contacts.

But New Zealand isn't where you make it big. If you're going to be anyone, you have to go to Downunder, to Australia.

Baxter made the move to Brisbane, Queensland, Australia and opened the Integr8 Gym. He marketed himself as one of the state's top fitness coaches with clients who played in the NRL and Australian Football League (AFL), and a host of other top Australian athletes. If top athletes in Queensland wanted to put on muscle in a way that supported their sports goals, they went to Rowan Baxter for his "functional bodyweight training" program.

Everything seemed to be going well for Baxter by 2008, but then his marriage fell apart.

Divorce is never good, but Baxter was able to separate himself from the situation relatively painlessly, although he did have a child with his wife. There were rumors of infidelity by both people and some said Baxter could be a little rough or even abusive, but he seemed to move on from the divorce with no problems.

Part of the reason for the easy transition was because he met Hannah Clarke.

A Shared Love of Fitness

Hannah Clarke was born in 1988 in the sunny and beautiful state of Queensland, Australia. Hannah was a good girl growing up. She never gave her parents many problems and never had the party scene phase so many teenagers do. In fact, Hannah was a bit of a health nut at a young age.

Hannah always watched what she ate, rarely drank alcohol, completely abstained from illicit drugs, and liked to exercise. By the time she graduated from high school, Hannah had morphed from an awkward adolescent to a very attractive young woman. She was trim, muscular, and with her long dark hair and brown eyes, she was a definite head-turner.

While most of Hannah's friends entered college after high school, she decided to work, and when she wasn't working, to work on her body.

Hannah liked fitness of all types, and she also liked to compete in various competitions. She was even the four-time trampoline champion in Queensland. Eventually, she began working in gyms and competing in Cross Fit, which is where she met Rowan Baxter.

When Hannah Clarke met Rowan Baxter in 2009, she was 19 years old and 11 years younger than the former professional rugby player. More importantly, she was much more inexperienced in the ways of the world than Baxter, which is partially what attracted her to him.

Baxter was definitely an interesting, worldly guy, but what really attracted Hannah to him was their shared love of fitness. The two began spending more and more time with each other at the gym, and out on the town, and after nearly three years of dating, the couple married in 2012.

Baxter proved to be a pretty good businessman, which allowed him to hire his new wife at his gym and for them to move to a nice new home in suburban Brisbane. By 2020, the couple had three children: Aaliyah (6), Laianah (4), and Trey (3).

Pictures show the Baxter family as a happy unit, enjoying the beach and other sights in Australia, but the reality is that things were far from perfect at home in Queensland.

Escalating Abuse

As with most relationships, the Baxter's enjoyed an extended honeymoon. But as time went on, it became apparent to many close to the couple that Rowan just wasn't the man they initially thought he was.

According to some of Hannah's friends, Rowan's abuse of Hannah was more psychological than physical. Although he was believed to have hit her on more than one occasion, Rowan apparently relied on threats and innuendos. He belittled Hannah when he didn't get things his way and if that didn't work, he threatened violence.

Rowan was the type of guy who got what he wanted, and when it came to his wife and children, that was usually the case.

That was, until 2019.

As Rowan's abuse against Hannah escalated, she decided to make a stand in late 2019 by taking the children and leaving Rowan. His response was to kidnap her the day after Christmas 2019.

The action could've - and in retrospect, should've - warranted some pretty serious charges, but since Rowan returned Hannah home unharmed, he was only hit with a domestic violence order.

The incident cost Rowan shared custody of his children, but once again, the courts relented and allowed him visitation.

But as all of this was happening, Rowan Baxter was seething with anger. He had lost total control over his family and essentially his life. When he learned that Hannah had taken back her maiden name, it was too much for him.

It signaled to Baxter that the marriage was definitely over and there was little he could do about it.

Well, Baxter made one last-ditch effort to win his wife back in early February, although it only resulted in him breaking the restraining order and losing all custodial rights to his children.

Rowan Baxter wasn't going to let this stand.

An Inferno of Hate

The backyard of Rowan Baxter's home in suburban Brisbane pretty much summed up where his life was headed in the days leading up to February 19, 2020. Clothing was haphazardly strewn on clotheslines, over lawn chairs, and on the ground.

The yard had the look of someone who no longer cared; someone who wouldn't be around any longer to take care of it. That's because at some point in the two weeks before February 19, Rowan Baxter made the decision to check out of life and take his family with him.

When Rowan Baxter woke on in the early morning hours of February 19, 2020, he apparently had a plan to put into action. He took a large knife from his kitchen, went into the garage and took a gas can he had filled prior. He got in his car and made the short drive to the Brisbane suburb of Camp Hill.

Camp Hill was where Hannah and the children lived. Rowan knew that if he got there early enough, he would catch Hannah taking the kids to daycare and school.

Baxter arrived at the home around 8:30 a.m. and saw Hannah and the children in her car. He quickly opened the door, showed the knife, and then did the unthinkable.

"He's poured petrol on me!" Hannah said to a neighbor as she tried to escape her crazed ex.

But before she could get away, Baxter lit a match and sent Hannah, their three children, and the car up in flames.

The neighbors who witnessed the horror were perplexed and had a difficult time processing what was taking place in front of them. In a matter of seconds, their quiet suburban neighborhood was torn apart by the worst kind of familial massacre one can imagine.

Some onlookers leapt into action after they got their bearings and realized what was happening, but a combination of the heat and Baxter keeping them at bay with his knife prevented them from helping.

And then it got even more violent.

Perhaps Baxter knew that he'd spend the rest of his life as a child killer in a tough, maximum-security prison. Or maybe he was content in an evil way knowing that he'd carried out his mission and that no one would ever have Hannah again, and that his children would never call another man "father." Either way, Baxter then turned the knife on himself.

When the paramedics arrived, Baxter and the children were declared dead at the scene but Hannah was clinging to life and rushed to the hospital. The doctors did what they could, but the damage was too much, and she died that night with more than 97% of her body burned.

As Hannah's family and people around Australia tried to make sense of the tragedy, Hannah's father perhaps summed it up best.

"The scum rots in hell. If he truly loved them, he would not have killed his children in such a horrible way," he said. "He might have said he cared [for] and loved his children, but I know it was always about him coming first."

CHAPTER 10

ANOTHER MURDEROUS UNCLE, THE LESTER STREET MASSACRE

Memphis, Tennessee is a tough city. It consistently has one of the highest crimes and homicide rates in the United States; it even beats many cities in developing countries. Street gangs and drug addiction are endemic to the city's north and south sides, but crime is never far from any neighborhood. The hipsters in Midtown and the students near campus can become victims just as quick as people in other neighborhoods.

So, in a city with so much crime and violence, it would take a crime of nearly unimaginable proportions to shock most Memphians. But that's exactly what happened on the night of March 2, 2008.

On that night, a career criminal named Jessie Dotson decided to take his frustrations out on his family. Like James Ruppert, Jessie Dotson wasn't a dad who killed, but he was the next worst thing - an uncle who killed.

And like Ruppert, Dotson turned his killing frenzy on two of his innocent nephews as well as his brother, his brother's girlfriend, and two other adults. Dotson also attempted to murder two of his other nephews and a niece but thankfully failed.

In a city accustomed to violence, it was the worst mass murder and familicide in its history.

The fact that six people were killed in one event was chilling enough, but once the local news reported that half of the victims were related to the killer, people in the Blues City were truly disturbed. You could say many Memphians have become jaded and somewhat accustomed to the drive-by shootings and drug deals gone wrong throughout the city, but family massacres were a type of murder that just didn't happen.

At least, they didn't happen until Jessie Dotson decided to become an uncle who kills.

Low Impulse Control

Jessie Dotson was born in 1975 in Memphis, Tennessee, and was raised in the tough Binghamton neighborhood on the city's north side. The Binghamton neighborhood is overwhelmingly black and poor and is plagued with many of the typical social and economic problems found in similar neighborhoods. It borders other neighborhoods that have higher Hispanic and white populations, but they too are poor.

In other words, Jessie Dotson's world was one where poverty, government dependence, and crime were the norms, but with that said, he still had options.

There are plenty of working people in the Binghamton neighborhood and many of the kids there graduate high school, get jobs, go into the military service, or attend the University of Memphis or other colleges.

But Jessie Dotson was never one of those kids who was interested in doing the right thing. To him, those kids were nerds, or better yet, "marks." Jessie did have big plans at an early age, but they all involved crime and violence.

Jessie emulated the drug dealers and gang bangers he saw daily on the streets of Binghamton. They were men who had money, women, and respect in a neighborhood that was often lacking in all three. The violence that came with the criminal lifestyle that those types of men lived also didn't bother Jessie. Young Jessie never knew his dad so he never really had any male guidance in his life, although it may not have mattered.

As a kid, Jessie Dotson became known for his short fuse and low impulse control. If someone rubbed him the wrong way, his first response was violence. If there was something he wanted, he took it, often violently.

Jessie's propensity to violence earned him quite the reputation at school, when he was there, and with the Shelby County juvenile court system. He entered the court system at an early age and like most juvenile offenders, learned that sentences were light if you were under the age of 18.

His reputation in the schools and courts gained him plenty of negative attention from teachers, school administrators, and probation officers.

He also gained the attention of the local chapter of the Crips.

Since Jessie aspired to the life of a career criminal on the streets of Memphis, joining a street gang was the next natural step. Being a gang member would give him protection from other violent thugs, and it would offer him new connections and resources, such as access to weapons, he normally didn't have.

After Jessie became a Crip, he dove even deeper into Memphis' criminal world by gang banging, drug dealing, and committing armed robberies. Although much of Jessie's early criminal behavior has been sealed by the courts since he was a juvenile when they happened, his adult court proceedings shone a light on enough instances that we can certainly fill in the blanks.

In 1990, when Jessie was 15, he was charged with misdemeanor disorderly conduct for threatening his mother. Mrs. Dotson had enough of Jessie's criminal activities and ordered him to stop, to which he responded by threatening to kill her.

It was only a month later when the Memphis Police pulled up to the Dotson home to bring Jessie to his mother. In this second incident, Jessie was arrested for assaulting a younger kid at school and attempting to extort him.

Jessie Dotson may not have been learning book knowledge as a kid, but by 1991 he was definitely learning quite a bit about life on the streets and how the legal system worked.

Despite the arrests, and his clearly being identified as a gang member, Jessie was allowed to continue with no real repercussions for his actions, or help for what were clearly psychological problems.

In the fall of 1991, Jessie then turned his wrath on his younger brother Cecil. Many boys who are older brothers have a naturally protective attitude toward their younger siblings, but any sort of feelings of familial love and fidelity were totally absent from Jessie. He assaulted his brother pretty viciously, which led to his mother locking him in a room and calling the police. When the police arrived, they found that Jessie had punched several holes in the walls.

But Jessie was just getting started.

The Memphis Police pulled over a car Jessie was riding in December 1991 that had a 20-gauge sawed-off shotgun and an unregistered .38 caliber pistol on the floor. Since Jessie was only 16 at the time and he wasn't the driver, he once more evaded doing any serious time.

And things would remain that way well into 1994 for Jessie. The young man showed no regard for others, even his own family members, and was willing to resort to violence in an instance.

All of this helped Jessie gain a reputation as a guy who "takes care of business" and someone to steer clear of if confronted. He used his reputation for violence to make major inroads in his gang and the criminal underground.

Jessie became especially adept at the art of the rip-off.

When he wasn't selling drugs on Tillman Avenue or out of his mother's house, Jessie would pass soap shavings off as crack cocaine. He usually got away with the ploy, as his victims were usually either too scared to confront him due to his violent reputation, or they didn't know where he lived.

On January 8, 1994, Jessie sold some soap shavings to a man named Halle Cox, but Cox wasn't just another one of Jessie's suckers. After discovering that the crack he just bought was really soap shavings, Cox found and confronted Jessie.

In a typical low impulse control fashion, though, Jessie responded by shooting and killing Cox.

The murder of Halle Cox went unsolved for several months, which is actually pretty common in Memphis. Memphis homicide detectives heard the name Jessie Dotson in their pipeline of informants and when they checked with the gang squad, they learned that he was an active thug in Binghamton.

The police arrested Jessie for murder in May 1994, but due to the fact that Cox was a bit of an unsavory character himself, and the eye witness testimony being unreliable, to say the least, the prosecutor allowed Jessie to plead guilty to second-degree murder on November 21, 1994.

Dotson was given an 18-year prison sentence.

The sentence meant that he'd do hard time in high-security state prison, but it also meant that he'd be back on the streets of Memphis one day.

A Murderer Comes Home

No one ever wants to end up in prison. It's obviously the end of the road if your life is heading in the wrong direction, but plenty of people use the negative experience to turn their lives around. Some people use prison as a chance to reconnect with family members they lost touch with or wronged. Many prisoners also use the time to learn new, legitimate skills or to get formal educations.

For Jessie Dotson, though, he wasn't interested in any of that.

The evidence shows that during the 14 years he spent behind bars, he only had one visit from family. The records also show that he barely spoke with them on the phone.

As Dotson was doing time, his family moved on without him. His brother Cecil followed his lead by becoming involved in a gang, although he joined a local chapter of the Gangster Disciples, which may have played a role in the events that later unfolded. After some brushes with the law, Cecil began straightening his life out by the mid-2000s, was gainfully employed, and had five children.

Jessie Dotson was an uncle, but he really didn't seem to care.

Instead of reaching out to family, Dotson decided to enmesh himself in the prison world. He navigated the world of the prison world well, floating among the rapists, thieves, and killers, and dealing with the Disciples, Bloods, Aryans, and Vice Lords on a day-to-day basis.

Dotson didn't do anything constructive when he was behind bars other than making more criminal contacts and further enhance his street cred.

And when he was paroled and returned to the streets of Memphis in August 2007, most people in Binghamton heard about it. Dotson immediately looked up a number of his old crew members, at least those who weren't dead or in prison, and then called his brother.

By all accounts, Cecil Dotson wasn't thrilled to hear from Jessie, but he was still his brother and since he was family, he agreed to see him. It proved to be the worst decision Cecil Dotson would ever make.

No One Was Safe around Jessie Dotson

Cecil Dotson may not have been the most responsible person earlier in his life, but by 2008 he was beginning to turn things around. He worked full-time as a maintenance man at an apartment complex and made enough money to rent a small house at 722 Lester Street.

It wasn't much, really. He shared the house with his girlfriend, 27-year-old Marissa Williams, and his five children—Cecil "CJ" Junior (9), Cedric (8), Cemario (4), Cecil II (2), and infant Ceniyah - yes things were a bit cramped, but they got by and Cecil generally kept the problems associated with his past life out of the house.

That was until his brother was released.

Jessie Dotson's nephews didn't really know him very well. They had never met him before he came to visit the house in January 2008, but they did know about him. They knew that he was in prison for doing something bad, but as is the case with most kids, they were non-judgmental and happy to meet their uncle for the first time in person.

Uncle Jessie didn't really reciprocate.

In fact, when Dotson was released from prison and back on the Memphis streets, he pretty much took over where he left off 14 years earlier by getting reinvolved in the criminal underworld. Although Dotson may have had the street cred from his stint in prison, he was somewhat of a relic of the past to most of the new generation of gangsters and dealers running the streets of Binghamton.

A few months after he was released from prison, Dotson went to Cecil's house to meet his nephews and spend time with his brother. Not long after his arrival, it became clear that even at 33 years old and after having spent nearly 14 years in prison, Jessie Dotson was still an angry, directionless person.

It probably also didn't help that he had been drinking heavily.

Instead of showing interest in his brother's family, Dotson was more concerned with telling prison war stories, trying to find out who was "running" things in Binghamton, and putting down his brother for being "soft." All of this continued for a few hours as the brothers and a couple of their friends played cards and drank a fair amount of booze.

91

Then when the card game was over, Dotson calmly got up from his chair, grabbed Cecil's jacket, and tried to walk out the door.

Cecil may have left the gangster lifestyle behind, but he wasn't a punk. He grabbed his brother's arm and told him to leave the jacket, but Dotson had other ideas.

He pulled out a pistol and told his brother to "take it."

Knowing his brother's history of violence and low impulse control, Cecil knew better than to challenge him, so he let him go. But he didn't let the matter go.

Cecil called the police and reported the incident.

The fact that Cecil reported the crime is important in this case for several reasons. First, it may have led directly to his and his children's murders. We know that Dotson had low impulse control, and on top of that in a neighborhood like Binghamton, the saying "snitches get stitches" is often true.

Second, the fact that Jessie Dotson never faced charges is also important. The Memphis Police apparently didn't have enough evidence to file charges, as it was essentially a case of "he said, he said", but the fact that a convicted felon was reportedly threatening someone with a gun should have warranted more attention. Even having a gun was a felony charge, never mind the threat and robbery, which were also felonies.

And even if the police didn't have enough evidence to charge Dotson, he was still on parole for his murder charge. His parole officer could have violated his parole for any number of reasons, the least of which was being around booze and gang members, which would have sent him back to prison for an indeterminate amount of time.

But instead, Jessie Dotson was allowed to remain free to commit a family annihilation.

"Uncle Jessie Did It"

It's unknown what Dotson did for the next month and a half after the confrontation at Lester Street, but he more than likely spent the time renewing his old business relationships in the neighborhood. Although Dotson's parole officer would have been justified in sending him back to prison, and it would have saved several lives, the reality is that he probably would have been difficult to find.

Dotson was listed as living with his sister and working as a painter with his father, Jessie Dotson Senior, but the streets have a way of hiding a person in plain sight.

Vanishing into the woodwork would've been easy for Dotson.

Although Dotson showed no signs of wanting to connect with his brother and his family, Cecil apparently wanted to bury the hatchet with his older brother. Younger brothers always do look up to their older brothers, no matter what they do, and there was every indication that Cecil wanted Jessie to be a part of his and his children's life.

So, Cecil reached out to his brother, telling him to come by the Lester Street house to make amends.

When Dotson arrived at the Lester Street house on the evening of March 1, 2008, the place was alive with activity. His brother and his brother's girlfriend were there along with their friends, 33-year-old Hollis Seals and 22-year-old Shindri Roberson. Dotson's four nephews and infant niece were also there, playing with each other and watching TV.

Dotson showed up at the house with his half-brother, William Waddell, to make it a family affair.

Dotson had been drinking booze throughout the day with Waddell, so when he arrived at Cecil's house, he was already intoxicated. He headed straight to the kitchen table where they'd had their card game that ended badly a month earlier.

CJ was happy to see his uncle, but Dotson wasn't interested. He only wanted to drink some more and confront his brother about being a "snitch."

The four adults in the house sat at the kitchen table, drinking and talking until the early morning hours. Although the situation was tense at first, things must have settled down because Dotson was there for several hours.

According to Waddell, who left between 10:30 and 11 p.m., everyone was still alive and all seemed well.

But then Jessie Dotson snapped!

Cecil said something that set Jessie off, and in a monumental display of no impulse control, he took his pistol out and shot his brother in the head. When the other adults started panicking, Dotson opening fire on each of them, dropping them to the ground one at a time.

It happened so fast that none of them even had a chance to run or attempt to disarm Dotson.

Then things got really sick.

Dotson later confessed that he thought about witnesses and that he, therefore, had to kill all of his nieces and nephews. So, since he was out of bullets, Dotson grabbed a couple of knives from the kitchen and went through the bedrooms stabbing his nephews one at a time.

As the oldest, CJ realized what was happening and tried to fight his homicidal uncle, but the violent killer's strength was just too much. The struggle ended in the bathroom where Dotson put a four-inch knife into his nephew's head and left him for dead.

Dotson then cleaned up and left everyone for dead.

Before leaving the house, Dotson attempted to stage the murders a bit. He found a shotgun and placed it next to Cecil to make it look as though he may have pulled a gun first. He also moved the adults' bodies around a bit to possibly give the impression that they were fighting among themselves.

It wasn't a real good or thorough job. He was never said to be the smartest guy, but the effort certainly shows premeditation.

Dotson attempted to go on with his life as if nothing had happened, even going back to work with his father on March 3.

But the mother of Cecil II knew something was wrong when she couldn't get ahold of Cecil. When Cecil's boss couldn't locate him, they called the police.

When the police arrived at 722 Lester Street, they were immediately taken back by the "smell of dead bodies," as officer Randall Davis said. After gaining entry into the home, they quickly found the deceased adults and as they went through the bedrooms, they found the children.

There was no way anyone could have lived through such a massacre, they thought, so they were amazed to find CJ and Cedrick clinging to life. Ceniyah was also severely injured.

Miraculously, though, all three of the children who survived the familicide eventually recovered. What makes it even more of a miracle is that the children lay dying in pools of their own blood for nearly 40 hours!

As with most murder investigations, the homicide detectives, who were featured investigating the case on an episode of *The First 48* true crime television show, focused on the family. Dotson was immediately a suspect, but it wasn't until CJ somehow told the police that "Uncle Jessie did it" that he was arrested on March 8.

He confessed to the murders, claiming that they took place after an argument and that he went after his nephews and niece to silence all witnesses.

Jessie Dotson was booked on six counts of first-degree murder and three counts of attempted murder. In Tennessee, he was facing the death penalty.

Waiting for Old Sparky

When Jessie Dotson finally went on trial for the Lester Street massacre more than two years later, he really didn't have much of a defense. He basically just claimed that someone else did it. His lawyer argued that any of Dotson's DNA found in the home was the result of him being a guest and that CJ's testimony was unreliable, considering the injuries he sustained from the vicious attack.

Dotson's defense did win a major victory before the trial began, though. They argued that because of the intense media coverage, Dotson wouldn't get a fair trial in Memphis. The prosecution countered that wasn't true and that every news station in the state of Tennessee had covered the case extensively anyway.

The judge more or less compromised, ruling that a jury of Nashville citizens would be seated for the trial in Memphis and sequestered.

Dotson even made the rare move of taking the stand in his own defense, but if anything, he demonstrated why criminal defendants never should do so. He denied the murders but got agitated and angry when the prosecutor pressed him about his violent past, his gang affiliations, and his tense relationship with his brother.

So, despite his attorneys' best efforts, there was just too much evidence stacked up against Jessie Dotson. He was found guilty on all counts on October 11, 2010, and sentenced to death the next day.

At the time of writing, Jessie Dotson sits on Tennessee's death row. Many people wonder if he'll ever sit in the electric chair.

Well, Dotson was originally scheduled to be executed in 2012, but the appeals process moved that date back to a now indeterminate time. Since Tennessee governor, Bill Lee, took office in 2019, there have been four executions up to 2021, which isn't that many compared to states such as Texas and Florida, but more than some other states.

It is of interest to note that, since the controversy over the use of the lethal injection method of execution sparked over the last few years, Tennessee switched back to using the electric chair.

As it stands now, Jessie Dotson will probably be the first notable uncle who killed to be executed by the electric chair, but it will probably be quite a while before it happens.

But not soon enough for many of the people in the Binghamton neighborhood of Memphis.

CHAPTER 11

DOING THE BOOKS AND KILLING HIS FAMILY

Boring...that's probably the one word that most people would've used to describe John Emil List in the days before November 9, 1971. List was a military veteran, a member of the Lutheran Church, and an accountant who had steadily moved his way up in the corporate world.

List also had three children, who by all appearances loved him. In turn, he was seen by everyone who knew the family as a good father.

John List even took care of his 84-year-old mother, Alma. The List family seemed to everyone to be the quintessential all-American family, living in a Victorian mansion in Westfield, New Jersey.

Like Robert Fisher, who struck 30 years later, John List was a man who lived for order and when the order of his life came crashing down in 1971, he decided that it was time to start a new life. After long, careful planning, John List coldly and efficiently killed every member of his family, one after another, on a cold November day in 1971.

On that day, John List died and Robert Clark was born.

As much as John List's familicide was horrifying, it was only the beginning of a nearly 20-year odyssey. In addition to both being control freaks, John List and Robert Fisher share the dubious honor of having evaded justice for quite some time for their crimes. John List was captured - thanks in part to the then-new television show *America's Most Wanted* - living a life that was as non-descript as the one he left.

When it comes to dads who kill, John List set the benchmark in terms of his kill count and ability to avoid capture. The John List case was so intriguing that it even provided the inspiration for the 1987 film *The Stepfather*, which is about an identity-changing dad who kills.

What makes the case even more fascinating is that John List would be the last person anyone would ever consider exciting or intriguing. But he was one of, if not *the most* notorious dad who killed in our book.

As Boring as You Can Get

John List was born in Bay City, Michigan on September 17, 1925. The city where List grew up, his family, and much of his early years were rather inauspicious, just like the way he usually portrayed himself to the outside world.

List grew up in a time when the country was undergoing some relatively big changes, which may have affected List later in life. As German-Americans, John's parents firmly had one foot in the Old World and another in America, which was actually quite common for the time, especially in the Midwest. List grew up with plenty of Germans, Polish, Czechs, Italians, and other assorted cultures in his Michigan town.

John's father, John Frederick, instilled in him a devotion to order that came straight from Germany but was tailor-made for the American Midwest. Along with devotion to order, John Frederick taught his son to be a pious follower of the Lutheran Church.

The adherence to order and religion probably helped the List family through the Great Depression relatively unscathed.

And like many young American men of his generation, John volunteered for the military after Pearl Harbor was bombed by the Japanese. John served in the Army in a non-combatant role as a laboratory technician and was discharged after the war.

But the order of military life appealed to List, so as he attended the University of Michigan in the late 1940s, studying business and accounting, he also took part in the ROTC program, becoming an officer in the Army.

List then faced the prospect of being sent to fight in the Korean War, but the Army saw his dedication to order and his education in accounting as a tool they could use so they assigned him to the Finance Corps...about as boring as you can get!

In fact, much of John List's early life until the mid-1960s was as unassuming as his looks. The tall, thin bespectacled List never had much of a presence when he entered a room, but he was also not offensive or annoying. You could say that he was pretty much just neutral. He was the perfect guy that many women were looking to settle down with in 1950s America, which is when he met his wife, Helen.

For Helen, John List was everything she was looking for in 1951. Her first husband had just been killed in action in Korea, so she was looking for something a little more stable and quieter.

Maybe even a man she could control.

She thought that the quiet and somewhat even mousy man would be perfect. And for several years he and their marriage were perfect.

The couple eventually had three children, and the family moved around the country a bit as John took some different accounting jobs. Both John and Helen were active in their church, and their children did well in school and were popular with other students.

But as John List watched his family from a distance, he noticed numerous cracks in his carefully constructed façade. Evil outside influences were threatening to destroy everything he had built, so it was his mission to do whatever he could to stop them.

Changing Times

John List was raised with the idea that if you worked hard things would turn out well for you in life, and by 1965 that seemed to be the case. He accepted a lucrative position as vice president of a bank in Jersey City, New Jersey that year, which allowed him to move his wife, three children - Patricia, Frederick, and John Junior - along with his mother into a spacious, 19-room mansion in upper-crust Westfield, New Jersey.

For List, it was the culmination of a life of hard work and an affirmation that the middle-class kid from Michigan belonged among the elite of the East Coast.

Always well-dressed in conservative attire, and often carrying a briefcase, the fastidious List seemed to fit right in with his upper-class neighbors as well, although he was also careful never to get too close to any of them.

John List was particularly adept at keeping people at arm's length, which served him well when he was on the run.

List and his wife were active with their local Lutheran Church and they were also very active in their children's school activities. But just underneath the surface, things were threatening John List's carefully orchestrated world of order. Things that were well out of his control.

As the Bob Dylan song of the era went, "the times they are a changing," yet List had no idea of how to deal with it.

The first major problem that List encountered in his well-manicured world was his wife. By the late 1960s, Helen had developed a severe mental illness that was aggravated by her heavy drinking.

And Helen was no happy drunk!

Perhaps driven by the booze, Helen had no problem disparaging John in public.

"She belittled him in public and always made a great hero of her previous husband, who died in the war," said Louis Grother, a former pastor of the

List's family in Michigan. "To compensate for that, he tried to do financial things for them. He got himself over his head in debt."

An autopsy of Helen List later revealed that she had syphilis, which she is believed to have contracted from her first husband. The disease was untreated, which led to her deteriorating mental state, blindness, and to her being bedridden. John never contracted the debilitating venereal disease because it becomes noncommunicable after a person has it for several years.

But it did wreak havoc on John's family.

Besides the tensions the disease caused due to Helen's erratic behavior and absence in most aspects of her children's lives, it probably did a number on John's psyche. After all, here's a guy who is used to complete control and who had a very strong - one could say rigid - moral code, so when he learned his wife was suffering from a venereal disease, it was too much.

To add to the chaos that was unfolding in List's life, he was fired from his lucrative job. He started his own insurance business but that proved to be a failure. List was rarely in his office, which only added to the family's increasing financial problems.

By early 1971, things were so bad that to keep things going, List took out a second mortgage on his home. He also took his mother's entire life savings of $200,000.

It still wasn't enough.

And to make matters worse, what List saw as the moral degeneracy of the counter-culture movement was seeping into his home.

His daughter Patricia, who was 16 in November 1971, was also disobeying him by ignoring curfew, hanging out with artists and hippies, and smoking marijuana and drinking.

By the fall of 1971, John List decided that he'd had enough. He'd had enough of the rat race, he'd had enough of his wife, and he'd had enough of the changing times. So, he decided to "opt-out" of things in his own kind of way, making the choice for his family in the process.

Saving Them by Killing Them

On the evening of November 8, 1971, John List knew what he was going to do the next morning. He'd thought about it quite a bit in the previous months and resolved to do it. He went to his study on the ground floor and took out his two pistols—a Steyr 9mm and a Colt .22 caliber. List made sure to clean them well. He couldn't have a misfire! He then loaded them, placed them in his desk, and went upstairs to bed.

The next day would be the most important day in John List's life.

It would also be the last day in the lives of all five of his family members.

When John List got up early in the morning of November 9, 1971, just as he had always done, he went straight for his study. He waited until his three children had gone to school and then emerged to carry out his carnage.

He started with his wife who was eating a piece of toast and sipping on some coffee in the kitchen. She didn't know what was coming. List killed her with a shot from the 9mm to the back of the head.

List then went to the upstairs apartment where his mother lived. He apparently surprised her in her kitchen because two bullets were found in the wall, indicating that she possibly tried to run. After killing the 84-year-old woman, List tried to drag her downstairs, but she was too heavy so he pushed her into a closet.

Apparently overwhelmed by adrenaline and emotion, List sat on his wife's bed before vomiting and then taking a shower. He then put on a suit and tie, as usual, and went downstairs. List then dragged his wife's body into the ballroom, leaving a 40-foot-long blood trail.

John List was now ready for phase two of his massacre.

List had written letters to his children's schools, the milkman, a few neighbors, and some other people telling them that the family would be in North Carolina for some time. He didn't want anyone getting suspicious about what had happened in the List home. After mailing the letters, he closed out the family's bank accounts and went home for lunch.

He then waited for his children to arrive home.

List was startled when he received a call from Patricia that afternoon. She didn't feel well and wanted him to pick her up from school. It presented a potential kink in his plan, but he had to get her so he drove to school, picked her up, and brought her home.

List made sure to go into the house before Patricia. He grabbed a pistol and waited behind the door for her to come in, then he shot her in the head before she realized what was happening.

Next was 13-year-old Frederick, who was killed by him, in a similar manner.

The final victim was 15-year-old John Junior, who caught wind of what was happening and tried to fight his murderous father. Although Junior fought back, John was stronger and armed with the .22, which he used to pump numerous bullets into his namesake until he was lifeless.

John then lined up all his family members in the ballroom in sleeping bags and cleaned the house. It wasn't that he was trying to get rid of the evidence - he admitted to everything in a letter - but it was probably his last attempt at instilling some order in his life that had so violently descended into chaos.

List then wrote a final note to his pastor, explaining why he had committed such an atrocity. The often rambling five-page letter attempted to biblically justify what he did, in part.

"At last, I'm certain that all have gone to heaven now," he wrote. "If things had gone on, who knows if that would be the case."

"Now they can die Christians," he added.

In List's demented mind, he was saving his family by killing them, but he would have to live in order to be redeemed.

In one final eerie footnote to the massacre, List made sure to rip his image out of every picture in the family photo album.

A month later, some of the neighbors thought it was strange that nearly all of the List mansion's lights had been on for a month straight. It was even stranger when the lights started to go out, so the police were called to the home on December 7.

When the police entered the home, they caught the distinct aroma of death. They also noticed how cold the house was: List had turned the temperature down to 50 degrees, presumably to lessen the stench of the decaying bodies.

Another strange detail was the classical music that was playing throughout the home in a repeating loop. List apparently wanted everyone to know that even as he committed an unspeakable act, he was still a man of culture and taste.

It was quickly determined that John List was the killer, and not long after they located his car at Kennedy International Airport in New York, but there was no record of him catching a flight.

It was as if John List vanished into thin air.

Starting Over Isn't So Tough

For most people, moving to a new city or state and starting a new job can be extremely difficult and stressful. The familiarity of the old job and home are replaced with the anxiety of learning a new job and reestablishing oneself in new surroundings. Many of you reading this have had to start over to a certain extent, so you know how difficult it can be.

Now imagine having to start over as a fugitive.

Mundane things that we all take for granted and that are needed to live normal lives, such as driver's licenses and bank accounts, suddenly became very difficult to attain. Some people have been able to thrive as fugitives for a number of years or even permanently. Most of those fugitives, though, were either career criminals who knew how to live outside the law, or outdoorsmen and survivalists who could live off the land.

John List was clearly neither one of those.

But John List was an intelligent man, meticulous in his planning, and quite resourceful when he needed to be. Among the evidence that the police found in List's home were a number of books about changing your identity and living as a fugitive, proving that List planned the family annihilation long ahead of time and he never had any intention of getting caught.

The authorities believe List first went to his native Michigan before moving on to the Denver, Colorado area, where he began using the alias Robert "Bob" Clark.

Starting over may be a tough thing for most of us, but even as a notorious fugitive John List/Robert Clark proved to be quite adept at starting a new life.

List first landed in Golden, Colorado, where he worked as a cook at a Holiday Inn. List kept to himself for the most part and spent his off days researching the city and building his identity.

"I didn't pry into his life, and he didn't pry into mine," said Gary Morrison, who was List's boss at the Holiday Inn. "He's the kind of person I trusted implicitly, and I still do."

Once List established his identity better, he felt more comfortable to start doing some of the things he did in his former life. By the mid-1970s, he was attending a Lutheran church in downtown Denver and by the late '70s, he was working as a controller at a paper box manufacturing company.

People generally liked Robert Clark, although they found getting to know him a bit tough. He continued to keep most people at arm's length and when they asked about his past, he usually offered little information. Sometimes he made mistakes and gave conflicting accounts, although apparently his very forgettable nature and personality made people forget the lies.

List also met Delores Miller in the late '70s through a single's group at their church. The couple married in 1985, and Delores was List's perfect complement in many ways: conservative, sober, and religious. List also continued with many of his pre-massacre interests and idiosyncrasies as he became more comfortable on the run.

He wore the same style wire-rim glasses that he always wore, and he continued to dress as he always had, well into the 1980s when wearing a suit and tie to do lawn work was long a thing of the past.

List also continued to indulge his love of classical music, history, and board games.

For a while, it seemed as though John List had recaptured the perfect life, he once worked so hard to build, but as with his first life, cracks were starting to form in the façade.

And this time the FBI was after him.

By the mid-1980s the world of accounting had dramatically changed. Any accountant worth their salt had to become acquainted with computers, but the ever-conservative List refused to learn the new technology so he lost his job.

List began doing taxes part-time for H&R Block to make ends meet, but it wasn't enough, so he cast a nationwide net for a full-time accounting job.

It was while List was living in Denver that his true identity was nearly revealed for the first time. One day his neighbor Wanda Flannery was in a supermarket when she noticed an article about John List. She thought that List looked an awful lot like Robert Clark, so she showed the article to Delores Clark.

For whatever reason, Delores threw the article in the garbage and it never came up again.

As the heat was apparently coming down on List, he gained a reprieve when he was offered a well-paying accounting job in the Richmond, Virginia area in 1988.

John List was once again on the move, staying one step ahead of the authorities. But as he got comfortable in Virginia, he became the focus of a popular new television show.

Hunted by John Walsh

In the mid-1980s, John Walsh was known in the United States for creating the nonprofit organization the National Center for Missing and Exploited Children (NCMEC). Walsh started the organization after his own six-year-old son, Adam, was abducted and murdered in Florida in 1981. Walsh was intelligent and articulate, but also had the persona of an "everyman", which helped propel the NCMEC to national prominence in a relatively short period of time.

In late 1987, the executives at the upstart TV network FOX created a true crime show that would profile notorious fugitives from around the United States called *America's Most Wanted* (AMW). Viewers would be given a phone number (and later an email address) where they could phone in their tips regarding the profiled fugitives.

The show was the perfect fit for the era. Other, similar shows, such as *Unsolved Mysteries*, which profiled fugitives in addition to the paranormal and other strange things, were extremely popular at the time.

In fact, the producers of *Unsolved Mysteries* considered airing a segment on the List case but ultimately decided not to, arguing it was too old.

But John Walsh decided to air a lengthy segment about John List in May 1989. He even hired forensic artist Frank Bender to make an age-enhanced bust of List. It proved to be a dead ringer and what led to the fugitive's capture.

As the List segment on *AMW* aired, back in Denver Wanda Flannery was watching with her daughter Eva and her son-in-law Randy Mitchell. The trio was amazed at what they were seeing.

"That's Bob!" They yelled in unison.

The three discussed and debated the issue for a bit. Although it was clear, or at least it seemed so, that Bob Clark was really John List, it was nearly impossible to comprehend. Bob Clark was such a mild-mannered, polite, and helpful man. He was god-fearing, church-going, patriotic, and the type of neighbor anyone would want.

But the more they discussed the situation, the more they realized that Bob Clark was in fact a notorious family annihilator, so they called *AMW* with the tip that led to his arrest.

When the FBI arrested List in Virginia, he initially stood by his claim that he was Robert Clark. Once his fingerprints were matched with those of the List home in New Jersey, though, he changed his tune.

Despite the mountain of evidence stacked against him, John List pleaded not guilty to the murders of his family members and decided to go to trial. His defense, if you could call it that, was that he suffered from obsessive-compulsive disorder (OCD), so he was legally insane when he committed the murders.

No one would doubt that List had a strong case of OCD, but so do millions of people in the country, and none of them meticulously murder every member of their family and then go on the lam for 18 years. The jury didn't buy it, finding List guilty of all five murders on April 12, 1990.

List was handed five life sentences and sent to the New Jersey Department of Corrections, where he died of pneumonia, alone and somewhat forgotten at the age of 82 on March 21, 2008.

Well, John List wasn't quite forgotten. The people of New Jersey will never forget what he did and he'll always serve as one of the most notorious examples of dads who kill.

CHAPTER 12

DUMPING HIS FAMILY INTO THE PACIFIC, CHRISTIAN LONGO

So far in our book, we've learned a few things about dads, and uncles, who kill. We've seen that they come from a wide range of social classes, can be found in different countries, and are not limited by race or ethnicity. It's also been shown that different motives drive these mass murderers, ranging from financial reasons to stress and even frustration.

As different as all these cases are, though, there are some similarities and threads of commonality that tie many of them together.

The idea of order, which we clearly saw with John List and Robert Fisher, and to a lesser extent with Jeffrey MacDonald, Steven Sueppel, and Yaser Abdel Said, played a key role in many of these familicides. All of these men were either raised with or developed a carefully constructed moral order, that if broken would bring chaos.

And we've seen so far what happened when chaos entered the lives of some of these types of men.

Christian Longo was another man who kept chaos carefully at bay for most of his life, but when it finally threatened his life, he reacted in the most violent way imaginable.

When Christian Longo had enough of his life, he simply tossed his family away into the ocean like they were garbage. He then went on vacation.

Thanks to numerous factors, not the least of which was Longo's inability to reinvent himself, Christian Longo was caught and faced justice. Many people familiar with Longo and the case think there was more they could've done to stop the massacre, but the reality is that it was impossible to tell when Longo was going to snap because he hid his problems so well.

Building a Façade

Christian Michael Longo was born in 1974 to a middle-class Jehovah's Witness family in Iowa but grew up in Ypsilanti, Michigan. If you're not familiar with the Jehovah's Witness Church, it's a non-Trinitarian Christian denomination that pursues a policy of missionary work, so there's a good chance you've met at least one at some point in your life.

Without getting into Jehovah's Witness theology too much, it is important to point out that they tend to be more socially conservative, opposing homosexuality, drug use, abortion, and heavy drinking. Although divorce is accepted, it is generally frowned upon.

The Jehovah's Witness Church is also very patriarchal, with men stressed as the leaders of their homes and the local congregation leaders, who are all men, being viewed as the patriarchs of their flocks.

So, as Christian Longo grew up in this faith, he was expected to fulfil its tenants in every way, and by all accounts, he did do that through his teens and into his early adulthood. After he graduated high school, Longo met his future wife, Mary Jane Baker, through the Jehovah's Witness Church. Longo was actually serving in the door-to-door ministry for the local church in Michigan and met Mary Jane one day in the church's parking lot.

The 19-year-old Longo and the 25-year-old Baker were immediately attracted to each other. And Mary Jane saw marriage material. In truth, Longo was just following what he learned as a kid and doing what he thought was expected; he probably should have been out dating and partying.

Instead, the couple married in 1993 and immediately started a family.

The couple had a son, Zachary, and two girls, Sadie and Madison, but it was clear early on that Christian was very immature and not a very good provider.

Christian Longo was a big dreamer who had many ideas to make money, yet he never put in the work needed to be successful. He was a manager of a newspaper distribution business and went from that to owning his own construction company.

Neither of the business ventures made Longo much money.

In fact, Longo began running up the family's credit cards and defaulting on loans. One of the family's cars was repossessed and bill collectors were constantly calling the Longo house. Seeing that he wasn't getting anywhere legitimately, Longo next turned to bank and credit card fraud.

Longo was eventually arrested for fraud, but since it was his first offense and the charge was non-violent, he was let off relatively easily with probation.

Needless to say, Longo's legal problems put a serious strain on his marriage, which was only made worse when Mary Jane learned he was cheating on her.

Although Mary Jane decided to forgive Christian and allow him to move back with the family, Longo's façade of a church-going businessman was all but destroyed. He was banished from his church and none of his friends wanted anything to do with him. With few other options left, Longo moved his family out of Michigan.

They first moved to Ohio and from there ended up in Waldport, Oregon in September 2001. Christian found a job at a local Starbucks while Mary Jane worked as a cashier at Walmart. Mary Jane thought that the move would be good for her family; they would get away from bad influences and soak up the scenery of the Pacific Northwest.

But Mary Jane quickly came to regret the move.

Was It All Planned?

The last time anyone saw Mary Jane and the Longo children alive was on December 15, 2001. According to Christian's own account, on the night of December 17, he sat up until late at night, stressing over his financial and legal problems. He had absconded from his probation in Michigan by moving to Ohio and then Oregon and would surely have to do jail time once caught.

And he knew it was only a matter of time until he was caught.

Longo decided - in a warped way that eerily echoed John List's massacre 20 years earlier and Robert Fisher's only months prior - that he was going to spare his family the suffering he caused and send them to Heaven early. With that said, the evidence seems to indicate that whereas John List truly believed that notion, Christian Longo just told the authorities that, to conceal his true, selfish reasons for wanting to eliminate his family.

Christian Longo was tired of being restrained by his family. He was tired of the constraints of his church, and he didn't want to deal with his impending legal problems.

So, on that cold December night, as his wife and youngest child slept in their beds and his other children slept in the living room, Longo decided to end his old life.

He calmly and coldly walked over to his sleeping wife and stabbed and strangled the life out of her. It took several minutes before he knew she was dead, and after that, he knew he'd crossed the point of no return.

Longo then strangled two-year-old Madison to death.

Longo may not have planned to kill his family on this night, but he had thought about it enough ahead of time that he knew what to do next. He went into the closet and got out two suitcases, a large one and a small one, and placed them in the living room. He then picked up Mary Jane's lifeless body and contorted her into the large suitcase.

It was much easier for him to put the tiny Madison in the smaller suitcase.

Before zipping up the suitcases, Longo put some exercise weights in with them. He then loaded each of the suitcases into the back of the family's 1999 Dodge Caravan.

It's believed that he then strangled four-year-old Zach and three-year-old Sadie, although it isn't known if he killed them in the apartment or at the dumpsite. Longo didn't put Zach and Sadie in suitcases; he tied them to cinder blocks.

Thankfully, he didn't tie them tight enough and he didn't use enough weight on the rest of his family.

Zach's body was found floating in an inlet of the Pacific Ocean on December 19, and not long after, Sadie's body was found. It had a pillow with a rock in it tied to her leg.

Then on December 26, Mary Jane's family had the worst Christmas in their lives when it was announced that she and Madison had been discovered floating near shore.

Of course, everyone was wondering: Where was Christian?

After the first two Longo children turned up in the ocean, the local police went to their apartment to investigate. Christian was long gone, but the police did find blood and other signs of struggle. They also began finding clues that pointed toward Christian planning the family annihilation for quite some time.

The place where Christian and his family were living in Ohio was actually a warehouse, and inside there were some pretty interesting things that the killer dad left behind. There were multiple books that documented how to create a new identity by stealing important personal information as well as books about changing your looks.

The police also learned that six weeks before the murders, Longo used his accumulated frequent flyer miles to take a flight from Portland, Oregon to

Sioux Falls, South Dakota to mail postcards from Mary Jane to her family to make it look like she was traveling.

Finally, it was revealed that Longo had stolen a credit card from a customer and used it to buy a one-way plane ticket to Cancun, Mexico. The police also found several social security numbers Longo had written down on a piece of paper, although he did not use them.

Within hours after murdering his family, Christian Longo was in Cancun, partying hard and living the high life.

Michael Finkel

Christian Longo always wanted to be something he wasn't. He had dreams of being a tycoon, and he also had dreams of being a world-famous writer. So, when he went on the lam in Mexico, he adopted the alias "Michael Finkel," professional writer.

Except Michael Finkel was a real person.

The real Michael Finkel had a few things in common with Christian Longo. Finkel wasn't a violent guy, but he was somewhat troubled.

In early 2002, Michael Finkel was at the top of the journalism world, writing for *The New York Times*, which earned him a nice paycheck and a solid reputation among his peers. But it all came crashing down for Finkel later that year when he wrote a story about the Arab slave trade in Africa using made-up sources.

Finkel was fired from the *Times* and his life seemingly began spinning out of control.

Christian Longo was familiar with Finkel's work before the writer was fired from the *Times*, so as he partied in the resorts, nightclubs, and dive bars in the Yucatan, he told everyone he was Finkel. Most people Longo met didn't know who Michael Finkel was, but more than a few recognized Christian Longo from the media attention in the United States. Plus, he'd been added to the FBI's most-wanted list on January 11, 2002.

If Christian Longo wanted to avoid capture as John List and Robert Fisher had done, he would've been better served by staying away from places popular with American tourists.

Longo wasn't on the most-wanted list long, getting arrested on January 13 in a small town about 80 miles south of Cancun. Christian Longo's brief life on the lam was over, but his trial was about to begin, opening a new chapter on this tragic case.

Longo was charged with four counts of capital murder, which meant he faced the death penalty if convicted.

Christian Longo's lawyers did the typical pretrial maneuvering for more than a year, leaving Longo with plenty of time on his hands. But before Longo even had a chance to formulate a defense with his lawyers, he was approached by disgraced journalist Michael Finkel.

Longo would finally get his chance to meet his favorite journalist.

The relationship between the two men was done purely through the mail for a couple of years, and the letters were pretty one-sided, at least to begin with, with Finkel doing most of the talking.

"The letters I wrote to Longo are some of the most open, brutally honest letters I've ever written," Finkel says.

Finkel had to get and keep Longo talking, and although Longo was facing trial and therefore tight-lipped, Finkel knew there was a story with the murders. But the trial proved to be another twist in this already very curvy case.

Christian Longo's trial began in March 2003 in a courtroom full of reporters and curious onlookers. Members of Mary Jane's family also attended the trial, as did Michael Finkel, who was using the material, along with the letters he received from Longo and the interviews he would conduct with him post-trial, to write his 2005 book *True Story: Murder, Memoir, Mea Culpa*.

The book was later turned into the 2015 film *True Story*.

But before James Franco would play Christian Longo in *True Story*, Longo had to go on trial.

It appeared to be an open and shut case, but in a final twist, Longo made the generally very rare decision among criminal defendants to take the stand in his own defense. Longo's defense was that Mary Jane killed the two oldest children and then he killed Mary Jane out of anger and self-defense.

So, what about Madison? He claimed that he killed her to save her the "pain" of losing her family. Years later, Longo admitted it was all a put-on show.

"I got up on the stand and essentially blamed my wife for everything. I was still stuck in a phase where I couldn't fathom the thought of me being capable of doing what I was convicted of," Longo said to an Oregon reporter.

Needless to say, the jury didn't buy the "self-defense" claim, finding Longo guilty of all four murders. He was then sentenced to death.

For Mary Jane's family, it was the best option available in an otherwise bleak and awful situation.

"I've never had an opinion about the death penalty. I have an opinion now. We will never rest until Chris is gone. We're not allowed to," said Mary Jane's sister Penny Dupuie.

But in Oregon, they may have to wait for quite some time, and as they do, it appears Longo will do his best to stay in the limelight.

Death Row Isn't So Bad

When Christian Longo received the death sentence, Mary Jane's family was comforted, although not necessarily happy, that Christian would finally meet some level of justice in this life.

Or would he?

As in all other states in the US that have the death penalty, all death sentences in the Oregon legal system go into an automatic appeals process.

But Longo really doesn't have to worry. Oregon is far from Florida or Texas when it comes to carrying out death sentences. The last person executed in Oregon was in 1997, and since that time, there's been a moratorium on all executions in the state. Based on Oregon's increasing move to the left politically, the state will more than likely eliminate the death penalty altogether at some point.

So, that means Christian Longo will probably never die in the execution chamber with a needle in his arm, but it does mean he'll spend the rest of his life in prison.

What kind of life is the former crook now living?

Well, inmates on death row at the Oregon State Penitentiary in Salem, Oregon are segregated in a cellblock with only death row inmates. They have free access to the unit from 6 a.m. to 9 p.m. and are allowed inside and outside exercise on the yards.

For amenities, inmates are allowed a TV, radio, and MP3 player in their cells, and have access to a wide variety of food, stationery, and other items from the prison canteen. Death row inmates are also allotted a certain amount of phone time each day.

Christian Longo has used his phone privileges to keep his name in the headlines and to feed his overinflated ego.

And Longo now admits that he has/had an ego that fueled just about everything bad he's done in life. You see, people in prison have a lot of time to think and in Longo's years behind bars, he's done some research and discovered that he's a narcissist...

Surprise, surprise!

In a letter to Oregon news station KATU, Longo claims he self-diagnosed his psychological disorder, writing:

"Studying what a psychologist said I was and came to terms with it, almost totally agreeing that he was right," Longo wrote. "His conclusion was the narcissistic personality disorder which he called 'compensatory'."

So, to overcome this disorder, Longo organized an organ donation campaign from behind prison walls.

Longo claims that the program is his way to partially make amends for the evil that he committed against his own family.

"I dream a few times a week about my daughters. They're usually happy and playing and it's pleasant. But my mind, even in the dream, knows the reality. And it always switches to an image of my son that haunts me for the rest of that dream state. Sometimes, I get back to sleep, a lot of times I don't."

Noticeably absent from Longo's dreams is his wife, Mary Jane.

Penny Dupuie isn't impressed with Longo's organ donation campaign and sees it as the killer's last desperate attempt to keep his name in the headlines.

"I have nothing for or against organ donation," said Dupuie. "But if this was truly important, there's a way to do it without going public on Facebook pages. If he wants to do something, do it quietly. He killed his own family."

Dupuie's anger and skepticism over Longo's motives are certainly justified, but she should rest assured that years from now after Christian Longo is long dead, he'll be remembered for his despicable acts as a dad who killed more than as an organ donor.

CHAPTER 13
THE CANADIAN CRIPPLER
KILLS HIS FAMILY

You're no doubt at least a little familiar with the "sport" of professional wrestling, or maybe you're even a fan. Hundreds of millions of people on every continent range from being occasional or casual fans of professional wrestling to diehard fanatics who pay big money to see their favorite wrestlers at live events and on pay-per-view shows.

I used quotes around the word "sport" because professional wrestling is not a sport in the traditional definition of the word. The matches are scripted with pre-determined winners and losers, with that being no real secret. By the 1990s most professional wrestling organizations really didn't hide the fact that their "sport" was "fake" in the sense that outcomes are fixed. Vince McMahon, the CEO of the World Wrestling Entertainment (WWE), formerly known as the World Wrestling Federation (WWF), the largest professional wrestling organization in the world, even calls his brand specifically "sports entertainment" and not a true sport.

Although professional wrestling may not be a sport in the traditional sense, you can't say that professional wrestlers aren't athletes. Or that they aren't tough.

Many professional wrestlers trained and competed as amateur wrestlers before embarking on professional wrestling careers, with NCAA champion Brock Lesner and Olympic gold medalist Kurt Angle being two of the most notable examples.

Other professional wrestlers include former professional football, basketball, and hockey players. Former powerlifters, bodybuilders, and MMA fighters have also stepped into the "squared ring" to try their hand at "wrassling," at it's known as in some places.

And you have to be quite an athlete to perform some of the feats of strength, high-flying maneuvers, and overall endurance that these men *and* women demonstrate daily.

In addition to top professional wrestlers usually having some type of athletic background and having to keep their bodies in top shape, wrestlers endure grueling schedules. Even the top card wrestlers, who are paid handsome salaries, have to travel extensively, wrestling in live events as many as six days a week.

Injuries are common.

So is a lack of sleep.

So, to compensate, professional wrestlers have often turned to pain killers to mitigate their injuries, amphetamines, and cocaine to get "up" for matches, and sleeping pills and "downers" to get sleep.

Most professional wrestlers have also done plenty of cycles of a variety of different steroids and many have drinking problems.

All of this has led to professional wrestlers dying at much higher rates than average; even higher than other professional athletes.

Most of the time, these troubled professional wrestlers are found dead in motel rooms, or at their homes, from heart attacks, strokes, or drug overdoses. Often, they are the only ones to die in these incidents, but in one notable case, the toxic drug cocktail that many professional wrestlers take led directly to a case of a dad who killed.

In 2007, Canadian professional wrestler Chris Benoit had the world in the palm of his hands. He had held multiple titles in all of the top wrestling organizations at the time and as a result, was financially wealthy and quite famous.

His star was set to rise even higher, but then on June 24, 2007, he snapped, killing his wife, child, and then himself. The tragedy sent the world of professional wrestling reeling, leading to investigations of drug abuse in the industry.

A French-Canadian Phenomenon

Chris Michael Benoit was born in 1967 in Montreal, Quebec to a working-class French-Canadian family. Chris grew up fluent in both English and French, and fully immersed in the Francophone culture of Quebec, but when he was still young, his family moved to the very different Anglophone Edmonton, Alberta.

The adjustment process didn't take long for Benoit, who found more opportunities in Alberta as a child.

Benoit was drawn to the world of wrestling in general as a kid, trying his hand at amateur wrestling. What he really wanted, though, was to be a professional wrestler. Chris grew up watching the Calgary-based Stampede Wrestling organization on TV and when he was just 13, he began training as a wrestler.

When he was 18, he traveled to the Canadian wrestling mecca of Calgary to try out for legendary wrestling trainer Stu Hart's training center known as the Dungeon. Some of Canada's greatest professional wrestlers trained in the Dungeon, including Brian Pillman, Lance Storm, and Hart's sons and nephews, most notably his son Bret "the Hitman" Hart.

After trying out for the Dungeon, Benoit was accepted for training. He turned professional at the age of 18 and by the late 1980s, he was wrestling in the top North American organizations of the era including the Atlanta-based National Wrestling Alliance (NWA), the St. Paul-based All-star Wrestling Association (AWA), and New York's WWF.

At 5'11 and 225 pounds, Benoit was slightly smaller than many of the top card wrestlers of the era, but he more than made up for his size with an exciting combination of aggression, technical abilities (on mat grappling and high-flying), and personality.

Usually pushed as a "heel" or "bad guy," Benoit had a way of getting under the fans' skin while winning their respect at the same time.

By the early 1990s, it was clear to most wrestling promoters that Chris Benoit was a legitimate phenomenon, but as with every professional wrestler, his "character" needed to be more fully developed.

Chris Benoit Becomes the Canadian Crippler

Today, the world of professional wrestling is dominated by one "big league," the WWE, but in the 1980s and into the '90s, the wrestling world was a patchwork of regional promotions. A wrestler could be a "face" (good guy) in the NWA one week and a "heel" in the AWA the next. For Benoit, this meant that he had plenty of work, but it also meant he traveled quite a bit.

He was known as the "Pegasus Kid" in Japan, wore a mask in Mexico, and was initially a "jobber" (basically fodder for the mid and top card wrestlers) in World Championship Wrestling (WCW), which was the successor to the NWA. Benoit had a difficult time "getting over" until he joined the upstart promotion Extreme Championship Wrestling (ECW) in 1994.

ECW was ahead of the wrestling times in many ways. It was still scripted, but its events were much more raucous, with more scantily-clad female "valets", much more violence, including regular use of chairs and other weapons, and an emphasis on its gritty, East Coast roots.

Benoit fit right in with the league and before too long he "got over." The ECW crowds loved to hate Benoit, who became known as "The Crippler."

Chris Benoit became famous for his crossface submission hold - which became known as the "Crippler Crossface" - his flying headbutt that he delivered from the top rope, and his devastating Supplex's. Benoit was respected by fans and other wrestlers alike for his in-ring abilities that combined raw strength, technical skills, and a little high-flying flair.

Benoit also developed a personality while at ECW.

Basically, Benoit portrayed himself as a surly thug with a thick Canadian accent. He learned to thrive off the hatred of the crowd and give it right back to them. And in no time ECW bigwigs noticed Benoit's skills and popularity, rewarding him with his first tag team title.

The bigger wrestling promotions also noticed The Crippler.

In 1995, Benoit was given a new contract with WCW, which was at that time challenging the WWF as the premier wrestling organization in the world. After some initial lackluster matches, Benoit was rebranded as the "Canadian Crippler" and joined the heel "stable" known as the Four Horsemen with legends Rick Flair and Arn Anderson.

From that point forward, The Canadian Crippler's professional life took a meteoric rise, but his personal life had its share of problems.

Love and Life on the Wrestling Circuit

As Benoit moved up the ranks in the professional wrestling world, he had some ups and downs in his personal life. When he found some initial success and started making some money, he married his longtime girlfriend Martina in 1988. The couple would have a boy and a girl, but the rigors of the wrestling lifestyle were just too much for the marriage.

Martina didn't want to be a wrestler's wife, and Chris had big dreams to reach the pinnacle of his profession. The couple divorced relatively amicably in 1997.

It's pretty easy for professional wrestlers to meet women. Just like rock stars, there are plenty of groupies who find their way backstage or to the wrestlers' hotel room. By the late 1990s, Benoit was involved with a woman named Nancy.

Nancy Toffoloni was quite familiar with the wrestling industry, having basically grown up with the profession and working as a ring girl, valet, manager, and wrestler since the age of 18. She eventually went by the ring name of "Woman," and became known more for her long dark hair, voluptuous body, and uncanny ability to help her wrestlers win their matches by any means necessary than for her in-ring wrestling.

Toffoloni eventually caught the eye of wrestler and booker Kevin Sullivan, and the two married in 1985. But even when both people are in the wrestling industry, wrestling couples seem to have a very finite lifespan.

Nancy hooked up with Benoit after he had divorced but while she was still married.

Nancy and Chris hooking up were actually part of a storyline that Sullivan wrote, leading many to joke that Kevin Sullivan "booked his own divorce," but the reality of what was really going on behind the scenes wasn't so funny.

By the late 1990s, the high-rolling lifestyle of professional wrestling was proving to be a double-edged sword for Chris Benoit. Although he appeared happy with Nancy and eventually married her in 2000, there were accusations that he was physically abusive.

Benoit also began experimenting with a plethora of different drugs during his ascent to the top of the wrestling world.

Because he was generally smaller than many of the biggest names in wrestling, Benoit felt the need to take a cocktail of steroids to put on muscle mass. He also had to take them just to keep up with the Joneses, as testing was rare in those days and wrestlers caught taking steroids were rarely punished. So, feeling he had to compensate for his relatively smaller size, he began taking more and more steroids.

But Benoit also began experimenting with the other drugs that are popular with professional wrestlers. Since injuries are a regular part of wrestling, and Benoit was sidelined by injuries on more than one occasion, he was introduced to different opioid-based pain killers. And since pain killers can bring you "down" and put you to sleep, Benoit also experimented with amphetamines and other "uppers."

He also took Xanax to relax and sleep from time to time.

By the early 2000s, Chris Benoit regularly took any number of drugs for a variety of different reasons. He wasn't necessarily addicted to any one particular drug or even class of drugs, and most of the drugs that he took were through prescriptions, but there was no doubt that he needed drugs in his system to function properly.

Yet as bad as Chris Benoit's personal life was becoming, he hid it quite well. He had a son with Nancy in 2000 and married her later that year. The couple seemed like the perfect, happy wrestling family. To top it all off, Benoit was making the biggest push of his career.

In 2000, no one would have guessed that Chris Benoit would become a dad who killed.

At the Top of His Game

Things changed rapidly for Benoit in 2000. First, his son Daniel was born, then he finally married Nancy, and later in the year, he joined Vince McMahon's WWE. The WCW had been beating WWF/WWE for months in ratings and winning the top talent, but finally, in late 2000, McMahon turned things around and defeated WCW once and for all. He had acquired most of WCW's top talent that year and in 2001 he would even buy the WCW name.

For Benoit, it proved to be a major boon to his career, but as was the case throughout his life, it also turned out to be terrible for his personal life.

Benoit won the WWE tag team championship in 2001 but was then sidelined with a serious neck injury. In addition to purchasing the WCW, McMahon also bought ECW, which meant that the WWE became much more violent, with chairs, ladders, and other weapons being used much more frequently in matches. This contributed to more and more injuries.

And in the Canadian Crippler's case, that meant more and more opioid abuse.

The injury also meant Benoit was spending more time in his family's suburban Atlanta, Georgia home, which normally could've been a good thing, but in the high-stress, drug-soaked lifestyle Benoit was leading, it turned out to be a nightmare for Nancy.

The couple's marriage quickly broke down and on May 12, 2003, Nancy filed for divorce from Chris, along with a restraining order.

"Chris had lost his temper and threatened to strike the petitioner [Nancy] and cause extensive damage to the home and personal belongings of the parties," part of the petition read.

The judge granted Nancy the restraining order, but three months later, the couple decided to reconcile and work on their problems.

When Benoit returned to work at the WWE, he was given a major "push" by Vince McMahon, which culminated in him winning the World Heavyweight Championship belt on March 14, 2004, at WrestleMania XX.

The other major title up for grabs at that event, the WWE Title, went to Benoit's friend Eddie Guerrero. The two men, who were close friends outside the ring, now celebrated their victories in the ring.

It should've been a joyous time for both men, but the reality was that they were both in the process of losing their fights with their demons, particularly drug addiction.

Although the Canadian Crippler lost his World Heavyweight Championship title, he continued to be a headliner in the WWE and won several other titles. With his career at an apex, he appeared ready to go even further, but then he was brought back down to reality a bit on November 13,

2005. On that day, Benoit learned that his best friend Eddie Guerrero had been found dead in a Minneapolis, Minnesota motel room.

The coroner ruled Guerrero's death to have been from heart failure caused by atherosclerotic cardiovascular disease, which was itself more than likely caused by years of steroid and amphetamine abuse.

Guerrero's death led to big changes at the WWE…. Well, sort of.

McMahon really couldn't hide the fact that the death of one of his biggest stars was the result of steroid abuse, so he instituted a new "Wellness Policy." Under the WWE's Wellness Policy, its talent was regularly tested for steroids and other illicit drugs, but there was a major loophole - wrestlers were allowed to take drugs with prescriptions.

This meant that most steroids were still acceptable, as were opioids. Cocaine use went down, but in its place, wrestlers started taking prescription amphetamines like Adderall.

The Canadian Crippler was able to continue his steroid use and even renewed a prescription on June 22, 2007.

A Toxic Mix of Pain Killers, Xanax, and Steroids

On the morning of June 22, 2007, the Canadian Crippler got into his car and made the 40-mile trip to visit Doctor Phil Astin III. Astin was Benoit's "guy," the same way drug addicts have a regular heroin or crack dealer.

Astin was Chris Benoit's steroid dealer.

Phil Astin was a legitimate doctor who had built a nice practice in suburban Atlanta. A large part of his practice was treating professional wrestlers, but his idea of treatment was putting the pen to his prescription pad. Once word got out that Astin was the guy to see if you needed some "juice" (steroids) or pain killers, his business really took off.

It was through word of mouth that Chris Benoit first went to Astin.

Over several years, Astin prescribed numerous prescriptions for Benoit, which was why the Canadian Crippler paid him a visit that day. After getting his ten-month supply of juice, Benoit drove back home.

At around six, before he left for the day, a pool cleaner saw the Crippler and his son barbequing. He later told the police that everything looked normal in the Benoit house.

The pool cleaner would be the last person to see anyone in the Benoit family alive.

It will probably never be known if Chris Benoit planned what happened next, or if he "snapped." But what is known is that, sometime in the evening, probably after Daniel had been put to bed for the night, the Canadian Crippler attacked Nancy.

The attack happened in an upstairs bedroom, which indicates it probably took place later in the evening as the couple was preparing for bed. An argument may have taken place prior or possibly Chris had it planned earlier. What is known, though, is that he quickly overpowered Nancy, bound her hands and feet with duct tape, and then strangled the life out of her with a TV cable.

It's unknown why the professional wrestler felt the need to bind his wife before strangling her. Although Nancy was quite athletic herself, she couldn't have offered much resistance to Chris.

Chris then wrapped Nancy in a blanket, put her on the bed, and placed a Bible next to her.

The Canadian Crippler next made his way to the opposite end of the couple's 7,500 square foot home to Daniel's bedroom.

What Benoit did next is debated by some, but due to the Xanax discovered in Daniel's body during the autopsy, it is likely that Chris woke him and had him drink some water spiked with the drug. Once the tranquilizer took effect, he strangled the life out of his helpless son. Then, as he did with his wife, Benoit placed a Bible next to Daniel's body.

It's not known if Benoit slept after killing his family, but he did make numerous phone calls the next day. He had already missed a couple of WWE events without calling in, but then made calls to his friend Chavo Guerrero, who is also the nephew of Eddie Guerrero. After playing phone tag with each other, Benoit and Guerrero finally had a short conversation on the afternoon of June 23, where Benoit said, "Chavo, I love you."

Benoit then wandered around his yard for a while before encountering a neighbor, who he told Nancy and Daniel were inside with food poisoning.

It was the last time anyone spoke with Chris Benoit in person.

Benoit then sent some texts to Guerrero and WWE referee Scott Armstrong, with what are now known to be instructions about locking the house and taking care of his dogs after he was dead.

Then in the early morning hours of June 23, Chris Benoit walked down to his basement gym, where he had spent many of his hours when he was home on the rare occasion. He looked at the lateral pulldown machine for a minute, took the bar off it, and fashioned a noose. Benoit then put the pin in the weight to the highest amount he could pull down. He sat down, put the noose around his neck, pulled the weight down with a towel, and then let go, hanging himself.

When Benoit failed to show up for a live WWE event on Monday, June 25, WWE officials called the Fayetteville, Georgia police to conduct a welfare check at the Benoit home. They found the bodies and a short suicide note that Benoit had curiously addressed to his first wife and the two children he'd had with her.

It was the greatest tragedy in the history of the WWF/WWE, and ultimately created more questions than answers.

Unanswered Questions

When the WWE learned of the massacre in the Benoit home, they dedicated their live TV show that Monday to the Canadian Crippler and had no live matches.

But then the reality of the situation set in.

I mean, after all, here was a guy who had brutally murdered his wife and child. As bad as it was that Chris killed Nancy, the murder of his own child was much worse. Wrestling fans questioned the WWE's response to the murders and before too long, investigations began.

The first and obvious question that people asked was: Why?

Were the murders planned well ahead of time?

Were the murders the result of 'roid rage'?

Were the murders the result of long-term traumatic brain damage?

Could the murders have been avoided?

The answer to the first question is still, and will probably remain, very much up in the air. After Eddie Guerrero died, Chris Benoit began keeping a diary, and in one entry he wrote, "I'll be with you soon," which certainly indicates that he at least contemplated suicide.

Another interesting statement was made by Nancy Benoit to one of her friends, who claims that a few days before her murder, she said, "If anything happens to me, look at Chris."

Both of these statements certainly verify what we know already - Chris Benoit was a very disturbed man - but they don't prove that he planned the murders of his family. Based on the evidence, or lack thereof, it's too difficult to say.

So, based on the lack of evidence of planning, many believe that the Benoit familicide was the result of 'roid' rage.

The term 'roid rage' is generally used to refer to bouts of violence or extreme aggression by people under the influence of steroids, most often long-term users. Since many steroids work by artificially increasing testosterone levels in the human body, and testosterone is a hormone associated with aggression, many have theorized that increased steroid use can lead to uncontrollable bouts of aggression, aka 'roid rage.'

The thing is, though, that plenty of people use steroids for many years and don't kill their families. As sports psychologist Sam Maniar said:

"It's really hard to say what comes first—it's like a chicken and the egg type of thing…. There's some evidence that mood changes can occur, but sometimes people have the rage or depression there before."

The final point to consider is if long-term traumatic brain damage led Chris Benoit to become a dad who killed.

As knowledge about traumatic brain injuries to former football and hockey players began to be examined in the mid- to late-2000s, some experts also started to look at how professional wrestlers are affected. Former professional wrestler Christopher Nowinski, who founded the Concussion Legacy Foundation, was one of the early advocates for wrestlers' protection from head injuries.

Nowinski noted that Benoit probably took more damage to his head than the average wrestler, as one of his signature moves - the flying headbutt - was a high-impact, high-velocity move that produced head trauma every time he did it. In addition, during Benoit's tenure with ECW, and as WWE later adopted the ECW's "hardcore" tactics, Benoit took many shots from chairs, clubs, and other weapons to his head.

A post-mortem examination of Benoit's brain by Julian Bales, the head of neurosurgery at West Virginia University, does seem to confirm Nowinski's theory.

In his report, Bales noted that "Benoit's brain was so severely damaged it resembled the brain of an 85-year-old Alzheimer's patient."

Finally, in terms of if the murders could've been avoided, that too is difficult to answer. Years of taking beatings to his head combined with constant steroid and drug abuse certainly contributed to Chris Benoit massacring his family, but in the end, the Canadian Crippler made the conscious decision to became a dad who kills.

CHAPTER 14

JAMES REID BAXTER, THE KIWI FAMILY KILLER

As we go through our catalog of dads, and a couple of uncles, who kill, we continually ask how and why they could commit such horrific acts. The act of murder is bad enough, the ultimate crime if you will, but killing children, especially your own children, seems to be especially unnatural. It is therefore logical for most normal people to wonder how one could do such a thing.

But as we've seen, there doesn't seem to be a simple answer in most cases.

Greed and the desire to get rid of one's old life appear to have played a role in some of these cases, namely those where the killer dads went on the run. Anger played a role in others, and sometimes even religion and culture may have influenced dads to kill.

But we've only touched briefly on a couple of cases where mental illness may have played a role, at least to the point where the killer dads were no longer legally responsible. The case of Purushottam Naidu may turn out to be one primarily driven by mental illness, while although James Ruppert's lawyers argued he was not guilty by reason of insanity, the courts ultimately ruled against the defense.

Our next case appears to be the one legitimate exception.

On the far southern tip of New Zealand's South Island is the small, sleepy city of Invercargill. Today, Invercargill is known as much for its nearby forests and beaches than anything, but in 1908, the region's rich soil and mild climate attracted farmers and those in the agricultural business.

One of those people was James Reid Baxter, who brought along his wife, and their five children.

The Baxter's moved into a small house in Invercargill in April 1907; a year later, they were all dead at James' hands. Despite clearly knowing who perpetrated the familicide, the local authorities did their due diligence and conducted a complete investigation, ultimately ruling that James was insane when he committed the crimes.

It was therefore one of the extremely rare cases of familicide where the perpetrator was deemed not legally responsible.

The "Invercargill Tragedy" as it became known, stands as one of the worst cases of mass murder in New Zealand's history, yet it is surprisingly often overlooked and has been given little attention in academic studies or by the popular media.

So, what really happened in Baxter home on April 8, 1908, and what drove James Reid Baxter to become a dad who killed?

A Businessman and a Family Man

Due to the limitations of record-keeping and technology in the 19th and early 20th centuries, many of the details about James Reid Baxter's life remain unknown, although we have a general outline.

James Reid Baxter was born in 1864 in England, which would have made him 43 in 1908. Before that time, though, not much is known about what Baxter did or when he exactly came to New Zealand. Part of the problem is that during the late 1800s, there was a great wave of emigration from England to other English-speaking countries. Many English immigrated to the United States, but most moved to countries still in the Commonwealth of the British nations, such as Canada, South Africa, Australia, and New Zealand.

New Zealand was the most out of the way of those nations, and the smallest, but there were still plenty of opportunities for industrious young men.

Baxter married his wife Elizabeth before 1887 and they eventually had five children, whose names and ages in 1908 were the following: Phyllis (11), Basil (9), Roy (4), Ronald (2), and infant John.

In April 1907, the Baxter's moved into a small house on Crinan Street in what was at the time the small town of Invercargill. James opened up a plant nursery business where he specialized in selling seeds to local farmers. It was a successful business and in no time the Baxter's were a respected family in the growing town. Among the friends they counted were Archibald McLean, a local missionary, and housewife Margaret McRobie.

The Baxter's were friendly and helpful and overall were considered good neighbors and members of the community. There were no accounts of James being abusive or even particularly strict toward his wife or children.

They were by all accounts a typical, happy middle-class family. There were no signs of anything to come and no clues that could've alerted neighbors, extended family, or authorities to act.

Yet not long after the Baxter's moved to Crinan Street, James' health took several bad turns that by all accounts played a major role in the later massacre.

Illness Strikes

Although 1908 is considered to be part of the "Modern Era" historically speaking, much of the technologies of that time would seem very pre-modern to us today, not the least of which in medicine. Antibiotic medicine had just been discovered and theories on mental health generally took the approach of "locking up" anyone with a serious mental illness.

It was for the most part unheard of for medical doctors to consider how serious physical illnesses could affect a person's mental well-being.

So, when James Baxter suffered a series of physical injuries and illnesses in early 1908, he didn't receive proper care, which ultimately played a role in his deteriorating mental state.

During the winter of 1907-1908, James caught a bad case of influenza, which kept him bedridden and out of work for a couple of weeks. The illness also left him physically weak, lowering his body's natural defenses against other diseases and injuries.

Then he contracted British cholera.

Unlike influenza, which is a virus, cholera is a bacterial infection that can be killed by antibiotic medicine. It is usually contracted by drinking water contaminated with fecal matter, which in 1908 New Zealand was not particularly uncommon. The human body has natural defenses against cholera and other bacterial infections, but since James Baxter was already weak from influenza, he was especially susceptible to the illness.

So, once again, James was bedridden for weeks and unable to work.

The illnesses that James suffered took their toll not only on his body and mind but on the finances and well-being of the household. To make things worse, Elizabeth was also suffering from illness at the same time as James, which made taking care of their relatively large family difficult.

Still, the Baxter family worked their way through the illnesses with support from each other and their neighbors. McLean and McRobie were both helpful neighbors, checking in on the family when they could and helping out when needed, such as by bringing them meals.

And just when it appeared that James' health was making a turn for the better, he was involved in an accident.

In March 1908, as James had all but recovered from influenza and cholera, he was 20 miles away from home in the town of Bluff on business. The details of what happened next are a bit scant, but it's known that James slipped on a rock on a cliff and took a nasty fall that left two large wounds: one on his head and another on his arm.

James refused to seek medical attention so he was once again bedridden, although this time his mental state was much worse.

Although James spent the next two weeks in bed, he rarely slept and hardly ate. His wounds also got infected, and by the start of April, he began acting erratically. Margaret McRobie later claimed that James stole a bottle of the opioid laudanum from her, and when she asked him to return it, he refused.

Baxter's erratic behavior continued. On April 4, he made a trip to a local hardware store, telling the owner that he was looking to buy a gun for rabbit hunting. The owner pulled out a nice new Remington .22 caliber rifle, which he said was perfect for the task. Baxter seemed to agree and bought the rifle. However, he returned two days later complaining that the rifle was too small to shoot the little animals.

The owner thought that Baxter's behavior was a bit strange - a 12-gauge would certainly be too large to kill rabbits - but since the "customer is always right," he obliged by exchanging the rifle for a 12-gauge shotgun.

Little did the hardware store owner know that James Baxter wasn't in his right mind and he had more nefarious plans for the shotgun.

No One Saw It Coming (Or Did They?)

It's difficult to say for sure if anyone could have predicted what happened next. Sure, James had suffered a number of health setbacks in the months before April 8, 1980, and those problems no doubt affected his financial and mental wellbeing, but he never exhibited any signs of violence. James Reid Baxter was never a violent man and even after suffering head trauma, he didn't appear to have turned into a violent man.

At least not immediately.

In the days directly leading up to April 8, none of Baxter's friends and neighbors noticed anything strange from the house other than John's ongoing battle with his numerous health maladies. The evidence shows that on the evening of April 7, all of the Baxter's apparently went to bed in their own beds as normal: Basil and Roy in the front bedroom, Phyllis and Ronald in the middle room, and the parents in the main bedroom with infant John in a cot next to them.

At some point in the late-night hours of April 7 or the early morning hours of April 8, James woke up still wearing his pajamas, put on a vest, picked up a 30-inch-long iron stove scrapper, and began to massacre his family.

It isn't known for sure the exact order that James did the massacre, but logic dictates that he began the assault in the front bedroom with Basil and Roy.

After quickly dispatching the two boys in the front of the house, James then went to the middle bedroom and beat Phyllis and Ronald.

He then only had his wife and infant son left.

Although the multiple attacks must have made some noise, Elizabeth apparently slept through it all, or at least most of it. The order of the attacks given here may have been reversed, though, with James attacking his wife first so she wouldn't awaken the children.

Whichever order the attacks followed, James killed his wife with repeated blows from the scrapper and then dispatched John with one blow to the head.

James then went into the bathroom and filled the bathtub. He grabbed his brand new 12-gauge, sat in the tub, put the barrel in his mouth, and pulled the trigger with one of his toes.

And so ended one of New Zealand's worst cases of familicide, but the investigation was just about to begin.

The Investigation

The Baxter family massacre was discovered the next day when neighbor Archibald McLean noticed a conspicuous lack of activity coming from the home. Despite suffering from numerous illnesses recently, James had been leaving every day to work at his nursery and the children could usually be seen coming and going to school or to play with each other and their friends.

On the morning of April 8, 1908, the Baxter home was eerily silent.

McLean peeked in and noticed the two children in the front room motionless on their beds, so he called for a policeman to investigate.

"I accompanied Sergeant Mathieson into the house, entering by the front window. We made a hurried examination of the two bodies in the front room and found life extinct. In the room immediately behind it, Roy was dead in bed and Phyllis was on the floor alive but unconscious. She was lying on one elbow and one hand with the other hand stretched out in front of the other. We next entered Mrs. Baxter's bedroom. As we went, in, she raised herself, turned towards the door and said 'What is the matter?'" said Archibald McLean.

Elizabeth, Phyllis, and John were taken to the hospital. If the event were to have happened today, they probably would have survived, albeit with scars and possibly permanent injuries. But as noted earlier, medical technology in 1908 just wasn't what it is today, and to make matters worse, Invercargill was a provincial town, far from Auckland or Wellington where the best surgeons and doctors practiced.

Elizabeth died on April 10 and John died on April 12. Phyllis, who wasn't expected to live more than a few hours, actually regained consciousness on April 11 but was paralyzed and had no recollection of the attack.

Without the needed medical care, though, Phyllis succumbed to her injuries on April 22.

The Baxter family massacre, which quickly became known as the "Invercargill Tragedy," obviously shook the rural community of the South Island and eventually all of New Zealand. No one could understand how a successful businessman could so brutally murder his wife and children, so the local authorities began a formal inquest.

It was quickly determined that James wasn't having an extramarital affair and that his business was financially sound - two of the more common motives behind or associated with familicide.

The fact that Baxter specifically bought a 12-gauge just days prior makes one think that he had originally planned to use it on himself, but the inquest almost immediately turned its attention toward James' mental state rather than any intent he may have had.

In addition to testimony from McClean and McRobbie, who noted how the numerous health and physical maladies James Baxter had suffered adversely affected his mental state, Baxter's employees at the nursery were also interviewed.

Employee George Carter said that Baxter had been suffering from depression for two weeks and that on the day of the murders he had complained about a bad headache.

Based on all of the evidence, the inquest ruled that James Baxter had suffered from temporary insanity and that "the other victims met their death while he was so suffering."

Clearly, the inquest believed that James Reid Baxter was a victim, but as soon as the findings of the inquest were made public, the massacre began to be forgotten about. The Baxter's were buried together in an unmarked plot in a cemetery in Invercargill and the case quickly dropped out of the headlines in New Zealand. You would expect to find at least a mention of the case in *Te Ara: The Encyclopedia of New Zealand*, which first came out in 2001, but it is silent. It's as if the entire country wanted to forget about the horrible incident and go back to building its image as a peaceful, quiet nation.

But something bad did happen in Invercargill, New Zealand on April 8, 1908, and just because the press quit reporting the story and the Baxter's were buried in an unmarked grave, doesn't mean that their names or their story should be forgotten.

CHAPTER 15

LOVING HIS FAMILY TO DEATH, BRYAN RICHARDSON

Copperas Cove, Texas is a city of about 30,000 people located right in the middle of the state not too far from Fort Hood. It's known for its mild climate, moderate crime rate, and close association with the United States Army. The area also played a role in the Texas War of Independence (1835-1836), but for the most part, it's a quiet place.

Most of the crime that does take place is drug-related and the violence that happens tends to be nothing out of the ordinary.

That was the case until December 12, 2020.

On that evening, the local police responded to a call that there was a potential domestic disturbance at an address. Domestic disturbances always have the potential of becoming violent, but on that night what officers found in the house will forever be seared in their minds.

Upon entering the home, they immediately found large pools of blood on the floor and when they entered a bedroom, they found 27-year-old Bryan Richardson covered in blood, lying in bed with his wife and two children. The police didn't immediately know if Richardson was a victim, but after a few seconds, they determined that the blood was that of his wife and children and that he had more than likely killed them.

Since at the time of writing the case is relatively new, Richardson is still in the early stages of the court process and details of the massacre are yet to emerge. Still, what is known about what happened that night is horrifying, as it involved a deadly stew of beer, pills, and anger, resulting in the worst familicide in the history of the small Texas town of Copperas Cove.

A Disturbed Dude

Although details of this case probably won't be fully released until trial, there are a few things we can glean from press reports. Richardson was married to a woman named Kiera Michelle in 2015, and the couple had two children, a son and a daughter. The daughter was attending a local preschool in December 2020. They lived in a working-class neighborhood of Copperas Cove at 1300 Fairbanks Street in a small but tidy house.

It's not the type of neighborhood where crime doesn't happen, especially domestic crimes, but homicides are rare and multiple murders are almost unheard of.

The few details that have come to light, though, paint the picture of Richardson being a mentally disturbed dude.

Richardson was originally from Virginia, but like so many people in recent years, he moved to Texas looking for better opportunities. He had worked at a local General Nutrition Center (GNC) store, but it appears that he had recently lost that job.

It isn't clear if he was laid off due to COVID-19 or for some other reason.

It's known that Richardson had been taking the drug Trazadone by prescription. Trazodone is a very strong antidepressant drug that is generally prescribed to combat cases of major depression, anxiety, and/or alcoholism. Since it is often used to counter the effects of alcohol withdrawal, and because it has sedative effects, trazodone should never be taken with alcohol, which Richardson was apparently doing.

In addition to, and probably because of his psychological and chemical abuse issues, there is evidence that Richardson's personal life was in a shambles.

It turns out that not only had Richardson lost his job, but he was also in the process of losing his wife and children too.

Apparently, it was all too much for him and he decided that he would never let his family go.

One Last Embrace

Although the police and prosecutors are still piecing together the details of what happened at Richardson's home on December 12, enough is known to build a basic chronology.

And it's very disturbing and very bloody.

Richardson was drinking during the day and finished at least one six-pack of beer, which combined with the trazodone he took proved to be a lethal combination. Not lethal for Richardson, though, but deadly for his wife and children.

The couple had an argument that was apparently bad enough for Kierra to call her brother Mark Santiago, but when Mark called back later, Kierra didn't answer.

Sometime in the early evening hours, as Richardson was under the influence of booze and trazadone, he grabbed a knife and stabbed Kierra dozens of times. It's unknown if the children witnessed their mother being murdered or if they were asleep.

It really doesn't matter, though, because if they were sleeping, they were awakened by the stabbing pain of a knife being repeatedly thrust into their tiny bodies.

Neither of the children had a chance.

Then for good measure, Richardson went into the kitchen and stabbed the dog to death.

What Richardson did next is truly bizarre, even among dads who kill. He dragged all three of the corpses into a single bedroom. He wrapped one child in a blanket and put her next to her mother. He then wrapped the other child in a comforter and placed him next to his sister.

Covered in blood, Richardson laid down, hugging his wife, and fell asleep.

Meanwhile, Santiago was extremely worried so he drove to Richardson's home. He knew that Richardson had problems and something told him that things were seriously off that night.

When Santiago got to the house, he noticed all the lights were off, so he shined a flashlight inside and noticed a dark-colored fluid all over the floor. He immediately called the police.

"I Already Lost All Those"

The police entered Richardson's home at 9:32 p.m. and immediately saw the dead dog in a pool of blood. With guns drawn, they called out the names of Bryan and Kierra, but there was no answer. They moved methodically through the small house until they got to a bedroom with a locked door.

They noticed blood seeping into the hallway from the room.

The police kicked in the door and were aghast at what they found. Richardson was lying there naked, covered in blood with his dead family. The police asked him what happened, but he only answered, "I don't know."

Richardson was arrested for murder and brought to the county jail for booking.

The forensic team came to the house to process the crime scene, taking away the bodies along with a knife, an empty six-pack of beer, and an empty bottle of trazodone. It was clear what the murder weapon was and at least part of what triggered the orgy of violence that night, but so many more questions remain.

And for the time being, Richardson isn't saying much.

Richardson has yet to admit to the murders, but when investigators asked him if he was afraid of "losing a job, his spouse, or custody of his children," his only response was, "I already lost all those."

Richardson was charged with three counts of capital murder and given a bond of $2.25 million. Since he's facing the death penalty, and since Texas regularly sentences people to death and routinely carries out death sentences, it will probably be another two years before Richardson goes to trial.

When this case finally does go to trial, no doubt new, bizarre details will emerge about this horrific crime and this killer dad.

CHAPTER 16

WHEN NEGLECT TURNS TO MURDER, JOHN JOSEPH YOZVIAK

We've profiled some pretty awful cases so far in this book. These men all murdered their families in some totally horrendous ways. None of these cases can be justified in any sort of way, but with most of them, you can't say these killer dads, and uncles, didn't feel anything.

Some of them had misplaced love that turned to jealousy and hate, while others felt their families were burdens. As awful as all of these men's crimes were, they still felt *something*.

Our final killer dad, though, apparently felt absolutely nothing for the daughter he is accused of murdering, which in some ways makes his case even worse.

In August 2020, 12-year-old Kaitlyn Yozviak died from a heart attack.

Yes, you read that correctly. A 12-year-old kid died of a heart attack!

That sounds strange because it is. There's no way a healthy child that age should die of a heart attack, and as Georgia state welfare authorities began investigating Kaitlyn's death, they quickly learned that she was anything but healthy. The poor girl was malnourished, was vitamin deficient, and worst of all was suffering from a long-term untreated lice infestation.

It was the lice infestation that caused the heart attack.

Due to the neglect, Kaitlyn's "father" 38-year-old John Joseph Yozviak, and her "mother," 37-year-old Mary Kathrine Horton, have been charged with second-degree murder. Although at the time of writing this case is still yet to go to trial - and therefore, more details are yet to emerge - this is clearly one of the worst cases of neglect inflicted by a dad on his child.

As awful as all these dads who kill are, they felt something. It appears that Yozviak felt absolutely nothing for his helpless daughter.

Definitely Not the Father of the Year

As with the Bryan Richardson case, this case is pretty recent and so Yozviak and Horton are still probably several months to two years away from trial, so many details are lacking. But enough details have emerged that point to the fact that neither should ever have been parents.

Yozviak and Horton are not married, although they have been together as a couple for several years, and Kaitlyn was their third child. The evidence shows that Yozviak has had problems providing for his family financially over the years, working a string of jobs and often moving his family to different homes in the Macon, Georgia area.

Despite having difficulties holding a job, or finding work that could really support a family, Yozviak and Horton had two sons in the early 2000s. Even with government assistance, they had problems taking care of the boys, who were often dirty and underfed.

Eventually, the Georgia Department of Family and Children Services (DFCS) got involved.

Although the Yozviaks moved around quite a bit in central Georgia, often traveling through multiple counties, DFHS kept getting reports and following up on them.

The reports of abuse at the Yozviak home were never physical or sexual but instead regarded neglect. Yozviak and Horton were never accused of doing anything directly to their two sons; it was just that they didn't seem to care.

After DFCS stepped in several times, the custody of the children was eventually contested in court. Mary Horton's mother, Anna, stepped in and was awarded custody of the two boys. Everything seemed well and for once it appeared as though the system had worked properly.

But then Mary got pregnant and gave birth to Kaitlyn in 2008.

Yozviak and Horton had no business having another child. They had to rely on the state to take care of Mary during the pregnancy, and it was clear to everyone that the soon-to-be-born child wouldn't have much of a life with her birth parents.

Yozviak and Horton at first agreed to give Kaitlyn up for adoption, but they changed their minds, which triggered another investigation by DFCS. Although Yozviak's home at the time was dirty, it wasn't bad enough for Kaitlyn to be taken from her birth parents. Birth parents have a right to their children and there's generally a very high standard that government agencies set for taking a child from their biological parents.

So, Kaitlyn Yozviak was left with her parents to weather the storm of neglect.

The Authorities Failed

This phrase is echoed quite a bit throughout the United States. Children are often left in abusive homes, especially when the abusers are their biological parents, with the end result being more abuse and, in the most extreme cases, death. Even in the cases where the child doesn't die, the socially unstable environment the child is raised in is usually passed on to the next generation.

With that said, there's only so much that county and state social workers can do. Laws restrain them, and unlike criminals, they have to - and do - follow them.

And sometimes, the failure to save children isn't entirely the authorities' fault.

After initially failing to take Kaitlyn after she was born, the DFCS had plenty of other chances, although most of them came after she was about ten years old. Before that time, Kaitlyn was a good student and was known to make friends easily. She even nominated one of her teachers, Courtney Williams, for a teaching award in 2016.

The DFCS received its first serious report of abuse in the Yozviak home in 2018 when they received a tip that Kaitlyn had been hit by a car but was never given proper medical treatment. When social workers arrived at the home, they were glad to see that Kaitlyn had not been hit by a car but they were disturbed at the condition of the home.

The house reeked of cat urine and trash was everywhere. Yozviak and Horton seemingly just put their trash in bags but never took the bags to the dump or burned them in their home, and there was apparently no trash pick-up.

Yozviak and Horton also seemed to be hoarders, as the junk was piled high throughout the house.

All of this legally rose to the level of abuse, but since social workers are generally tougher on physical and sexual abuse, Yozviak and Horton were given another chance. They spent six days cleaning the home from top to bottom so that when the social workers returned, they found things noticeably improved and cleaner.

But this was only a temporary bandage on what was a gaping wound.

Social workers were called to the Yozviak home on other occasions, but since there was no physical or sexual abuse, the parents were given warnings and told to clean the premises.

The number of complaints probably would have eventually triggered a more complete investigation or resulted in Kaitlyn being given to her grandmother, but when COVID-19 hit in early 2020, things dramatically changed. The schools shut down so kids with problems were no longer regularly observed by teachers and other officials. In Georgia, tips on child abuse to state and county authorities dropped by 50%.

And Kaitlyn Yozviak was among that statistic.

Head Lice Can Actually Kill

For Kaitlyn Yozviak, there was no Skyping or Zooming with her teachers and classmates when the COVID restrictions hit. She was relegated to her dirty home and her life of neglect, where no one would have any idea of what was happening.

At first, neighbors regularly saw Kaitlyn playing outside, but by the summer, she was rarely seen.

Kaitlyn was also rarely bathed.

The shack that Kaitlyn shared with her mother and father in the small town of Ivey, Georgia only fell into a worse state during the COVID restrictions. Yozviak and Horton apparently didn't mind living in filth, and among rodents, because the house was so infested with rats that they scurried over Kaitlyn as she slept.

But, as bad as the rats and general filth were, the head lice that Kaitlyn contracted proved to be deadly.

Head lice are fairly common among children, who like to play in dirty places and rarely like to bathe or shower. With that said, head lice infection is also easy to treat. Prescription shampoos can kill the lice and their eggs with a couple of easy treatments, so in the year 2020, there should be no reason for anyone to have a major head lice infestation or for it to continue for months.

But that's what happened to Kaitlyn Yozviak. When she was brought to the hospital on August 26, 2020 with cardiac arrest, lice bites were ruled as the major contributing factor.

Lice bites will lower iron levels in the human body, and when a lice infestation is allowed to continue, it can cause anemia, which can lead to death.

After Kaitlyn's death was reported to the authorities, the Georgia Bureau of Investigation (GBI), the state's investigative and police organization, got a warrant to search the Yozviak home. They were amazed at the level of filth they found. After investigators compared the autopsy report with what they found at the home, they determined that Kaitlyn suffered from "excessive physical pain due to medical negligence" and that her parents were the cause of her death.

John Yozviak and Mary Horton were both charged with second-degree murder and child neglect for Kaitlyn's death. Chances are both will spend considerable time in state prison, where they will no doubt be much better cared for than their neglected daughter.

CONCLUSION

Among all classes of criminals in the world, dads who kill are considered by many to be the worst. Criminals in general, and even murderers, can be written off as "bad seeds" and aberrations in a society where most people are law-abiding.

But how are we supposed to view men who kill those they are supposed to protect?

How are we supposed to judge those with little or no paternal instinct?

These questions can be answered by reading the 16 cases in this book. As awful as the crimes of these dads and uncles were, the judgment they have received from society is equally as harsh. Humans generally see murder as the ultimate crime, so when a father murders his own children, it's considered especially bad. And make no doubt about it, familicide is *seen* by most people as a truly disgusting, if not the *most* disgusting, of all crimes.

Yet as universal as people's disdain and disgust is toward dads who kill, this book has demonstrated that the dads who kill are not necessarily a "one size fits all" group.

There are, though, a few patterns that emerge and some sub-groups that these dads can be placed into.

First, there are the dads who kill because they wanted to be free of their familial obligations. Christian Longo, James Ruppert, Robert Fisher, Steven Sueppel, Anthony Todt, and possibly Jeffrey MacDonald fit into this category. Some of these men were carrying on extramarital affairs, while others were involved in crimes and financial scams, but all wanted out of the lives they had. Some, such as List and Sueppel, tried to justify their actions by stating they were sparing their families from shame, although the reality is they were driven by personal desires and greed.

We also examined some cases where religion was carried to an extreme or misinterpreted extent played a role in familicide. John List, Marcus Wesson, Purushottam Naidu, and Yaser Abdel Said were all killer dads for whom religion played a major role in their lives. These men also used their religions to justify their murders, although many are quick to point out that they twisted legitimate religious beliefs to meet their warped world views.

Envy, the cause of so much strife throughout world history, was apparently one of the major contributors in the cases of the two murderous uncles we profiled. James Ruppert and Jessie Dotson were two very different men, but they shared envy of their brothers and their families. Neither of these men had an uncle's love for their nieces and nephews, and both were willing to massacre them to get back at their hated siblings.

Finally, traumatic brain injury and mental illness probably influenced the familicides perpetrated by Marcus Wesson, Chris Benoit, James Reid Baxter, and Bryan Richardson.

As of the time of writing, Richardson's case is still to go to trial, but so far, the evidence seems to indicate that he wasn't playing with a full deck. Wesson demonstrated over the years that he too was not the picture of sanity, yet how much of that was self-induced remains a subject of debate.

Benoit and Baxter, though, may have had more legitimate arguments in defense of their insanity. Both men suffered brain trauma before they committed their horrible acts, and as scientists learn more about traumatic brain injuries, it very well may turn out that - among all the cases in this book - these two were the most avoidable.

So, what does our journey through these 16 cases of dads who kill tell us about the nature of familicide?

It's clear that dads who kill can come from any ethnicity, strike on any continent, and are not restricted to any socio-economic class. Dads who kill, are driven by different motivations and while many of them choose to join their families in death, some go on the lam, and others are arrested.

About the only thing we can say with certainty about dads who kill is that, unfortunately, it's only a matter of time until the next major case grabs the headlines.

MORE BOOKS BY JACK ROSEWOOD

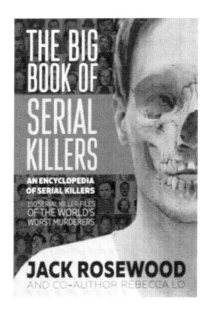

There is little more terrifying than those who hunt, stalk and snatch their prey under the cloak of darkness. These hunters search not for animals, but for the touch, taste, and empowerment of human flesh. They are cannibals, vampires and monsters, and they walk among us.

These serial killers are not mythical beasts with horns and shaggy hair. They are people living among society, going about their day to day activities until nightfall. They are the Dennis Rader's, the fathers, husbands, church going members of the community.

This A-Z encyclopedia of 150 serial killers is the ideal reference book. Included are the most famous true crime serial killers, like Jeffrey Dahmer, John Wayne Gacy, and Richard Ramirez, and not to mention the women who kill, such as Aileen Wuornos and Martha Rendell. There are also lesser known serial killers, covering many countries around the world, so the range is broad.

Each of the serial killer files includes information on when and how they killed the victims, the background of each killer, or the suspects in some cases such as the Zodiac killer, their trials and punishments. For some there are chilling quotes by the killers themselves. The Big Book of Serial Killers is an easy to follow collection of information on the world's most heinous murderers.

Our first volume caused such an impact that we've decided to bring you the long-awaited Volume 2 of the most comprehensive Serial Killer encyclopedia ever published!

Murderers or monsters, normal people turned bad or people born with the desire to kill; it doesn't matter where they come from, serial killers strike dread into our hearts with a single mention of their names. Hunting in broad daylight or stalking from the shadows, we are their prey and their hunt is never done until they are caught or killed.

With a worrying number of them living in our communities, working alongside us at our places of employment and sharing the same spaces where we spend time with our families, serial killers are typically just another neighbor that we barely think about. A worrying thought, to be honest.

In The Big Book of Serial Killers Volume 2 we go through the lives of 150 serial killers who allowed themselves to fall under the influence of their darkest desires and took the lives anywhere from one to one hundred victims; we speak of their motives and how their stories ended (*if* they ended...), and remind you of the fear and pain that they left behind.

But what can you expect from **The Big Book of Serial Killers Volume 2?**

You will find such things as:

- An excellent A-Z list of all of these deadly killers, allowing you to reference the encyclopedia whenever you need to find out more about any single murderer.
- All of the uncensored details of their crimes, with much effort taking into account to describe their horrific acts.
- Important information on their date and place of birth, date of arrest and number of victims, among other facts.
- A list of Trivia facts for each killer, allowing you to learn more about their personalities and any films or documentaries made about them.

So, with nothing more to add – it's only time now for you purchase this book and begin learning about 150 of the sickest, most dangerous serial killers in world history.

This is the next level in murder: are you ready to learn about the evilest men and women in history?

Made in the USA
Las Vegas, NV
12 November 2023

80695274R00094